Managing Business Tenants

706

by

Gary Philpott MA (Cantab), AITP, ACIArb, Solicitor
and
Garry Hicks BSc, ARICS, ACIArb

IE

1994

Estates Gazette

A member of Reed Business Publishing

The Estates Gazette Ltd
151 Wardour Street, London W1V 4BN

2 1 APR 2009

ISBN 0 7282 0203 4

Typesetting by Amy Boyle Word Processing, Rochester, Kent
Printed by Bell and Bain Ltd., Glasgow

Contents

Tenant failure

Checklists

Preface

This book is aimed at all professionals involved in business leases including property managers, accountants, banks, surveyors and lawyers. It is a start and not an end. It is intended to put any professional with a commercial lease problem on the right tracks to a practical solution.

We thought initially that producing the preface would be the most fun part of the text. An opportunity to reflect on the text and to make poignant comment.

Two matters then became apparent.

The first was that most would be unlikely to read it anyway; especially the busy practitioner at whom the text is aimed.

The second is that this will be the only opportunity both of us would have to thank those to whom we are indebted for putting together the text.

From Veale Wasbrough thanks must go to Mandy Merrick for typing most of the text and to various colleagues including Hugh Barraclough, Anne Ebery, Julie Exton, Martin Howe and Tim Smithers for their help and comments on the material.

From Chesterton thanks must go to Teresa Pine and Paul Winteringham.

Gary Philpott
Veale Wasbrough
Orchard Court
Orchard Lane
Bristol BS1 5DS

January 1994

Garry Hicks
Chesterton
Queens Avenue
Clifton
Bristol BS8 1SB

Table of cases

Table of Cases

Table of Cases

ix

Table of statutes

Table of Statutory Instruments

EXISTING AND NEW TENANTS

CHAPTER 1

Tenants and businesses to avoid

1.1 Introduction – good and bad markets

In a good market, rental income flow is assured. In bad or poor market good property investment focuses more and more closely upon the quality of the tenants or in property-speak, 'covenant strength', and landlords realise that securing the best possible tenant overall is preferable to taking the highest rental bid regardless of all else. Landlords are often willing to forego immediate income return in preference for a sustainable tenant company that will form a solid and reliable cash flow generator. Little time need be devoted to identifying the most preferred tenants who in the main will be household names or subsidiaries of the major plc's.

The following sections, however, concentrate on identifying those businesses to "treat with caution" and some of the tests to apply when considering new tenants, either by way of direct lettings or assignments of existing leases.

1.2 Undesirable covenants

It is difficult, if not impossible to generalise. The quality of covenant which can be expected depends heavily upon the type and quality of property under consideration. Prime high street shopping pitches attract prime high street retailers. Tertiary parades servicing neighbouring shopping needs do not.

In difficult market circumstances where new tenants are scarce, the property manager must weigh up the benefits of creating and maintaining cash flow against the type and quality of tenant he would ideally wish to secure.

It is the property manager's task to satisfy himself on a proposed tenant's creditworthiness and standing before proceeding, and the following investigations and precautions should be considered.

1.3 Company and credit search

When dealing with a tenant of reasonable size, a search should be obtained from an organisation such as Dunn & Bradstreet which consists of two parts:

1. The financial strength of a business.
2. The composite position.

The financial strength indicator reflects a company's tangible net worth. It is derived from the most recent audited financial report and accounts. When present, intangibles such as goodwill, patents and research costs are deducted from the net worth.

The composite position or risk indicator is the second part of the rating and reflects a company's financial health, stability and overall condition.

The following and other data are used to determine the appropriate indicator code:

1. Sales trends
2. Profit trend
3. Working capital
4. Payment score
5. Tangible net worth
6. Worth
7. Bank opinion
8. Indebtedness
9. Industry norms
10. Public notices
11. Antecedents
12. Payment score

There are four ratings: strong, good, fair and poor.

1.4   References on new tenants

In all cases except "blue-chip" companies, at least three references should be obtained, one of which must be a bank reference and one from a previous landlord if possible. The reference must refer to the total amount of the estimated outgoings under the lease, not just the rent.

The hierarchy for bank references, subject to minor variations between organisations is as follows:

1. "Undoubted" – very seldom given, but covers the best "blue-chip" company.
2. "Considered good".
3. "Should prove good".

4. "Customers resources appear fully utilized, but would not undertake any commitment he could not fulfill" – the bank has known the customer for some years and has had a satisfactory relationship. However, the customer has commitments and would not be able to pay for instance, under a guarantee immediately, and the bank may have to fund him further.
5. "Unable to speak for your figures" – unacceptable.

The use of references in relation to the landlord's legal right to refuse consent to an assignee (as opposed to the new tenant) and whether that is reasonable, is dealt with under Chapter 4 – The protection measures for the landlord.

1.5 Trading accounts
Unless the tenant company is a well known and substantial public company, it is usual to request at least a copy of the last year's and preferably the last three years' trading accounts. Trading accounts can be referred to an accountant for an opinion, but the following simple checks are useful:

1. *Turnover and profit*: identify the ratio between the two to give the return on sales (ROS). A ROS below 10% is questionable.
2. *Fixed assets* – in particular identify if possible freehold property as these assets might provide the ultimate fall-back if the tenant goes into liquidation:
3. *Rent cover* – crudely, the net trading profit of the prospective tenant company after deducting director's remuneration should not be less than 2.5 to 3 times the rent reserved under the lease.

1.6 Rent deposit and personal guarantor for new tenant
If the previous tests leave any residual doubts about the prospective tenant but you wish to proceed with the letting, then the use of a rent deposit is the preferred safety net, with a personal guarantor providing a secondary fall back. In really doubtful cases it is better not to proceed with the letting rather than have an elaborate system of, guarantors and rent deposits.

1.7 Rental deposit
The deed dealing with the deposit must specifically provide that the money belongs to the landlord, preventing any receiver or liquidator laying claim to it. The terms of the deed are dealt with further under

Chapter 4 – Protection measures for the landlord.

The deposit money should be placed in an interest bearing account of the landlord's choice and in the landlord's name. Interest will usually accrue to the tenant and will be payable to him at agreed intervals.

The terms of the deed should provide, if possible, for the rent deposit money to be used not only in the event of tenant's liquidation, but also if the rent is not paid or if there is a breach of the tenant's covenants.

1.8 Personal guarantor for a new tenant

It is of no practical benefit to have a personal guarantor who is a man of straw and the reference procedures detailed earlier must be followed to assess his credit-worthiness and standing.

The guarantor should be resident in the UK and subject to the jurisdiction of the English courts. He must give a permanent address for service of notices or proceedings.

The appointment should be irrevocable except with the landlord's consent. Preferably the personal guarantee should be for the full term of the lease. If it is restricted to the period of occupancy by the particular tenant, then provision should be made for substitution of guarantors in the event of an assignment.

CHAPTER 2

Difference between new leases and assignments

2.1 Granting a new lease

When a landlord is granting a new lease he has a free hand as to the terms of the letting and of the security he is entitled to seek from his tenant – the only limitation being market forces.

Among the matters which the landlord should consider when granting a lease are the need to protect and enhance the value of his assets; to limit his financial exposure; and to optimise his cashflow.

For example:

- Would it be better for the rent to be payable monthly rather than quarterly?
- Is it possible to obtain "on account" contributions for service, charge/insurance premium?
- Ensure that the tenant must pay interest on overdue payments.
- Ensure that items such as insurance premium and service charge are recoverable as rent, so that the "fast track" remedies available for rent arrears may be available.
- Ensure that the lease entitles the landlord to recover legal and surveyor's costs in pursuing the tenant for breaches of covenant, including rent arrears.
- Where the landlord is letting out part of premises, ensure that the tenant assumes direct liability for rates, and that separate meters are installed for electricity, gas, etc.
- Pass all repairing liability on to the tenant either by direct covenant or comprehensive service charge.
- Where the landlord is itself a tenant and is granting a sublease, ensure that dates for payment by subtenants precede payment dates under the headlease – eg if rent under the headlease is due on March 25, consider a rent day of March 1 to assist in cashflow. Likewise with rent reviews – you never want to face a negative profit rent.

Not only does a landlord granting a new lease have complete freedom as to the terms on which he lets property, he also has a free hand in choosing his tenant.

2.2 Granting consent to an assignment of an existing lease

Given that most leases are granted for 25-year terms, the landlord is frequently asked to give his consent to the assignment of an existing lease to a new tenant. From the practical point of view, the landlord will seek to avoid a prospective assignee who is less secure than the previous tenant, and accordingly might damage the value of the landlord's interest in the premises – ie the higher the risk of the tenant proving impecunious, the lower the value of the landlord's investment.

An original tenant remains liable on the covenants contained in his lease for the whole of its term even though the lease may have been assigned.

The lease will almost invariably provide that the landlord must not unreasonably withhold its consent to the assignment. The ideal protection is therefore tempered by what the landlord can justify as being "reasonable". This is a question which has been before the law courts on numerous occasions.

The difficulty is that there are no hard and fast rules, and the "reasonableness test" must be applied to the individual circumstances of the ingoing tenant, and by reference to the existing protection the landlord may already enjoy. How this test operates in practice and the statutory control under the Landlord and Tenant Act 1988 are more fully dealt with in Chapter 3 on the licence to assign.

2.3 The need for flexibility

In a poor property market there is over-supply, matched by paucity of demand. This results in a decline in market rental levels, often significantly below the passing rents on existing leases, which were either granted or subject to rent review during stronger market conditions.

As a consequence many tenants find themselves contractually bound to pay rents substantially in excess of current market rental values. Over-rented property is likely to be a feature of such a poor market and therefore fund management and investment strategies must be reorientated to accommodate such a poor market if it arises.

The standard institutional lease in the majority of cases precludes tenants from assigning or subletting their accommodation at anything less than the reserved rent under the lease. Additionally, there is often a prohibition against assignment for a reverse premium. Not surprisingly most landlords are worried about permitting new rents at anything less than the established rent on their property due to the adverse impact not only on rent reviews (and hence the landlord's rental stream), but also upon the perceived capital value of that investment.

The risk for inflexible landlords is that the tenant may either go into administration or receivership or even worse, into liquidation. All of these will have a severe impact on the landlord's cash flow and it may well be prudent to accommodate a tenant's request to assign or sublet and maintain the bulk of the income flow rather than place the entire income in jeopardy.

CHAPTER 3

Licence to assign

transfer

The assignment of a lease has to be completed by way of a deed (section 52 of the Law of Property Act 1925) and this applies whether or not the lease itself was by deed. There is no statutory requirement for the landlord's consent to the assignment to be given by deed, but the practice is to give such consent by way of a formal licence to assign prepared as a deed.

The objective from the landlord's viewpoint is to obtain a promise or covenant from the new tenant to pay the rent and to observe and perform the covenants in the lease throughout the rest of its term. The effect of the covenant is to create a contractual link between the landlord and the assignee which will last after that assignee has passed on the lease. Each assignment will therefore increase the landlord's security, making each assignee, effectively, a guarantor for the remainder of the term of the lease in the same way that the original tenant is liable for the whole period of the lease.

The reason for this practice of employing a formal licence to assign arises from the doctrines of privity of estate and of contract. The original tenant is liable for the whole period of the lease by virtue of the doctrine of privity of contract: the lease is a contract between the original tenant and the original landlord and each remains liable to the other so long as the lease continues. Subsequent assignees are only liable while they hold the lease under the doctrine of privity of estate. The licence to assign therefore creates a continuing contractual link between an intermediate tenant and the landlord; and ensures such intermediate tenant remains liable after it has parted with the lease. Many assignees who have long since passed their leases on, have found themselves in the unenviable position of having the provisions of such deeds enforced against them in the wake of company failures by subsequent assignees.

It is for this reason, primarily, that consent from the landlord to any assignment of the lease should be given by formal deed.

The first issue which the landlord will need to consider is whether his consent is required to the proposed assignment. If so, then whether to give consent. If the landlord does not wish to give consent, the next issue is whether he is entitled to withhold consent to the proposed assignment.

If the lease does not provide that landlord's consent is needed for the tenant to assign, then the tenant may assign the lease without making application to the landlord.

3.1 When to withhold consent

If the lease provides that the tenant may not assign the lease or that it may not assign without landlord's prior consent then the extent to which the landlord can control an assignment is as follows:

- If the lease includes an absolute prohibition on assignment the landlord need not give his consent to a proposed assignment. However, it is still within his power, in effect, to vary the terms of the lease by agreeing to waive that prohibition. Indeed, he can require a premium payment as a precondition to giving consent.
- If the lease provides that a tenant may not assign the lease without the landlord's consent, (ie a qualified prohibition) then the landlord may not unreasonably withhold consent (section 19 of the Landlord and Tenant Act 1927).
- If the tenant may not assign the lease without the landlord's consent, it is also implied that the landlord will not require payment of a fine or similar payment as a condition for that consent being given; although the landlord can require the tenant to pay his reasonable legal and other expenses in dealing with the consent and the preparation of the licence to assign (section 144 of the Law of Property Act 1925).
- If the landlord's consent is required to the assignment (or indeed if there is an absolute prohibition on assignment and the landlord is prepared to consent to a waiver of that prohibition), then the landlord cannot withhold consent on the basis of the race or sex of the tenant or proposed assignee, except in relation to certain residential premises (Sex Discrimination Act 1975 and Race Relations Act 1976).

The remaining issue for the landlord is whether in withholding consent he is acting reasonably. There were a number of guidelines set out in the case of *International Drilling Fluids* v *Louisville Investments (Uxbridge) Ltd* [1986] 1 EGLR 39 and, although not all of them are now relevant, following the enactment of the Landlord and Tenant Act 1988, these guidelines remain relevant:

- That the object of the obligation on the tenant not assigning without consent is to protect the landlord from use or occupation of the premises in an undesirable way.
- That the refusal by the landlord has to be related to his relationship with the tenant as such and to the lease and that grounds that are not related to this are unreasonable.
- That there may be situations where the difference between the benefit to the landlord and the detriment to the tenant in the landlord withholding consent is such that refusal would be held to be unreasonable.

In addition to the above principles, there are a number of situations in which the court has decided that it would be reasonable to withhold consent.

Some examples are:

- Where the proposed assignee's financial standing is in doubt, particularly if there are well-founded doubts as to the proposed assignee's solvency.
- If the assignee will be put into a better position than the assignor, for example by acquiring security of tenure.
- Where the assignee is certain to be in breach of the terms of the lease on taking the assignment.

Where the current tenant is not the original tenant, the landlord's refusal of consent to an assignment by the current tenant to an assignee may still be of concern the original tenant. As the original tenant remains liable for the whole period or term of the lease, an assignment to an assignee in circumstances where the financial stability of that assignee is in doubt, may result in an increased risk of action by the landlord against the original tenant should that assignee fail.

However, the landlord is under no implied duty, at law, to that original tenant, to take any care to ensure that an assignee is financially able to meet the rent and other payments due under the lease *Norwich Union Life Insurance Society* v *Low Profile Fashions Ltd* [1992] 21 EG 104.

3.2　Landlord and Tenant Act 1988

The Act imposes further controls on the landlord forcing him to act expeditiously if an application for consent to an assignment is made by a tenant. Failure to act quickly and to supply reasons for any withholding of consent exposes the landlord to risk of a claim for damages from the tenant.

The duties on the landlord are as follows:

- To give consent to the proposed assignment within a reasonable time unless it is reasonable not to do so.
- To serve on the tenant notice in writing of the decision whether or not consent is given and setting out in addition any conditions to which that consent is subject.

The Act applies wherever the lease prohibits the tenant from assigning, subletting, charging or parting with possession of the premises without the landlord's prior consent.

Anyone who receives an application in writing from a tenant to consent for such a transaction, also owes the tenant a duty to make sure that reasonable steps are taken to pass on the application.

The burden of proving whether the consent has been reasonably withheld now rests on the landlord under section 1(6) of the Act. By section 1(4) if the landlord gives consent subject to unreasonable conditions, then, for the purposes of the Act, that is treated as unreasonably refusing consent: see *Midland Bank plc* v *Chart Enterprises Inc* [1990] 2 EGLR 59 as an example of this principle in action. The reasonableness of any refusal is judged by the known circumstances at the date and time of the decision to refuse consent: see *CIN Properties Ltd* v *Gill* [1993] 37 EG 152.

However, no fixed limit has been placed on what constitutes a reasonable time in which to respond to an application from a tenant for consent to an assignment and it will still, as a matter of fact, depend on the circumstances of the case: see *Hick* v *Raymond & Reid* [1893] AC 22.

The practical problem for the landlord is how to respond quickly to an application for consent to an assignment to comply with the Landlord and Tenant Act 1988, while protecting his interest in the premises.

An action plan might be as follows:

- To acknowledge receipt of the application speedily and to set out in that acknowledgement what further information is reasonably needed by the landlord to come to a decision whether or not to give consent to the assignment. A pro forma may help.
- To notify the tenant shortly after the acknowledgement, whether that further information has been received, setting out how and

when the consent will be given and if so, the conditions to which such consent is subject. In particular, that the consent is subject to completion of a formal licence to assign.
- To follow up any further information received from the tenant and any queries on the conditions quickly.

The points for the landlord to remember are:
- To give consent subject to an unreasonable condition is deemed to be a refusal (section 1(4)).
- To refuse to give consent where the tenant, on completion of the assignment, would be in breach of the lease is reasonable (section 1(5)).

Since the emphasis in the Act is on speed of response it may be worthwhile for the landlord to give the tenant time-limits and provide a timetable as to how soon he needs the further information to make the decision and how quickly he would be able to respond: the object being to set up an early dialogue between the landlord and the tenant as to what would be a reasonable time in which to deal with the issue of consent.

3.3   Key terms of the licence
The object of the licence to assign is to create a contractual link between the landlord, the current tenant and the assignee on the terms on which the assignment is made.
The key obligations will be:

- An agreement by the landlord to give consent to the assignment from the existing tenant to the assignee for the residue of the term of the lease.
- A covenant by the assignee that, as from the date of the assignment, he will be responsible, during the residue of the term of the lease or any continuation or extension of it, statutory or otherwise, for the rent and for the performance and observance of the other terms and conditions in the lease.
- A covenant by any guarantor of the assignee that, throughout the remainder of the lease, the assignee will pay the rent and comply with the other terms of the lease, in default of which the guarantor will pay such rent and comply with such terms.

However, there is a risk that requiring the guarantor to guarantee the performance of the lease for the remainder of the term, as opposed to the period during which the assignee is the current tenant, may be held to be unreasonable: *Evans* v *Levy* [1910] 1 Ch 452.

Where the consent to the assignment is tied in with the change of use of the premises then the landlord may want to impose on the assignee the following further obligations:

- To obtain and produce to the landlord all necessary consents required by statute or byelaw for the new use
- To pay to the landlord any increase in insurance premium arising from the change of use.
- To indemnify the landlord against claims arising from the change of use.

There is, unless the lease states otherwise, no duty upon the landlord to be reasonable when dealing with an application for change of use and he can refuse without reasons. He can always trade consent for a change of use for other concessions. Note however that he cannot require payment of a premium for giving consent to a change of use: see section 19(3) of Landlord and Tenant Act 1927.

3.4 Reform: priority of contract

The position of the original tenant and subsequent assignees has been considered by the Law Commission (report number 174, 1988). If the report's proposals are implemented, they will have a dramatic effect on the licence to assign in future leases. This topic is dealt with in Chapter 19.

CHAPTER 4

Protection measures for the landlord

The protection measures that are considered below are primarily concerned with the issues that arise when a landlord is looking at a prospective assignee. The main issue in that context is whether it is reasonable for the landlord, where he has power to do so, to refuse consent to the assignment and the evidence for that consent, or refusal will depend on the strength of references, trading accounts, available guarantors and/or rent deposits. In relation to new tenants these issues have been covered above under Chapter 1 – *Tenants and businesses to avoid*.

4.1 References

The topic is dealt in relation to new tenants under Chapter 1.4.

The first form of evidence the landlord receives as to the tenant's status is likely to be references – usually from the proposed tenant's bank, his accountant or solicitor, a previous landlord and some trade or other credit references. References are usually couched in terms that the referee regards the prospective tenant as responsible and trustworthy, but excluding the referee from any liability for his opinion. The courts have generally indicated that a landlord need not give much weight to such superficial references: *British Bakeries (Midlands) Ltd* v *Michael Testler & Co Ltd* [1986] 1 EGLR 64 and *Ponderosa International Development Inc* v *Pengap Securities (Bristol) Ltd* [1986] 1 EGLR 66.

The best that can be said of references is that they may give a general guide as to the tenant's standing and certainly the absence of a reference, or a reference that is equivocal should prompt the landlord to make further enquiries.

Although not strictly a point on reasonableness, it is worthwhile emphasising that a landlord letting to a company tenant should always carry out a search at Companies House to establish background information about the tenant, including, if filed, previous accounts.

As to the question of reasonableness and references, it will always be appropriate for a landlord to ask for references, except possibly where the tenant is a High Street name of national reputation.

4.2 Trading profits

If strong references are not available (or even if they are) a landlord will generally be justified in asking for copies of the proposed tenant's trading accounts. Several recent court decisions demonstrate that some level of profitability may reasonably be required by the landlord so that he can be satisfied that the tenant will be capable of paying the rent. The leading case is *British Bakeries (Midlands) Ltd* v *Michael Testler & Co Ltd* [1986] 1 EGLR 64 where evidence was given that a generally accepted test of the financial standing of any proposed tenant is that its accounts show a pre-tax profit of not less than three times the amount payable under the lease in question.

Although this case has provided a "rule of thumb" its approach was questioned in *Venetian Glass Gallery Ltd* v *Next Properties Ltd* [1989] 2 EGLR 42. In that case the assignee was a company with relatively poor trading figures which was increasing and improving its trade at a rapid rate. In that case the court found that the traditional approach took too narrow a view of the responsibility and respectability of the proposed assignee. Landlords must therefore give some weight to the immediate prospects of the assignee though it is submitted that these prospects must be judged realistically and not simply on the basis of the tenant's grand projections.

The need to consider sureties and rent deposits will only apply if strong covenants are not available and, as a matter of law, it is reasonable to require further protection.

4.3 Guarantor covenants

Guarantor covenants (or surety covenants) generally contain a number of provisions which are accepted as "standard". There are, however, three which may be highlighted as being important (and in most cases reasonable) to include, namely:

- The guarantor must be a principal debtor (ie he must be equally liable for any breach of the tenant's obligations and not simply liable if, and to the extent that, the tenant is unable to make good a particular breach. Also his obligation must survive the tenant's death, insolvency, etc.

- The guarantee should extend not only to performance of the tenant's covenants, but also to taking a new lease if the lease is disclaimed by the tenant's trustee in bankruptcy or liquidator.
- Provision should be made for substituting guarantors if the existing guarantor dies or becomes insolvent.

Unless specifically limited, a guarantee will last throughout the rest of the lease, even if the new tenant subsequently assigns. Guarantors may therefore seek to limit liability to the obligations of their own company, or may seek a release when trading profits reach a certain level. Whether such qualifications are reasonable is again a matter of applying the legal test in the particular circumstances.

Although the availability of a surety is influential, it is not a substitute for an adequate tenant. This principle was reaffirmed in the case of *Warren* v *Marketing Exchange for Africa Ltd* [1988] 2 EGLR 247. There may, however, be cases where the reverse applies, such as where there is a new company with no track record, but the individual behind the company is plainly committed to the success of the new company's business and is able to act as guarantor.

4.4 Rental deposit

The idea of a rent deposit is that the tenant places a certain amount (eg three or six-months' rent) into a separate fund against which the landlord may draw to recover any deficiencies in rent payments, or the cost of remedying other breaches of covenant such as repair.

The deposit agreement usually includes the following arrangements:

- Interest on the deposit is due to the tenant (subject perhaps to the landlord retaining a certain percentage as an administration fee).
- If a tenant breaches the lease, the landlord may withdraw funds from the deposit and immediately call on the tenant to restore the deposit to its original value.
- If there is a rent review, the deposit must be increased proportionately by a further payment from the tenant.
- If the landlord assigns his interest, he may also assign the benefit of the deposit.
- If the tenant assigns the lease, arrangements are made either for the tenant to recover the deposit or for the landlord to retain it –

thereby leaving the tenant to seek reimbursement from his assignee.

- Tenants will very often seek to include provisions whereby the deposit becomes repayable – such as where their trading profits in three consecutive years exceed three times the rent payable. The landlord may find it hard to resist such an amendment in the light of decided cases indicating that where an ingoing tenant can establish such a financial performance, it is unreasonable for the landlord to seek further security.

If the tenant is a company and the rent deposit deed amounts to a charge over the fund, it should be registered at Companies House. Failure to do so may render it void as against a liquidator.

CHAPTER 5

Impact on investment value

5.1 Property investment characteristics

To understand the impact of the quality of the tenant's covenant upon an income-producing property it is useful to examine the features which give property its characteristics as an investment.

Commercial property is a different investment medium to the more conventional and widely-understood securities traded on the stock exchange. These characteristics include:

- It is not an "off the shelf" investment such as shares in British Telecom. Property investors have to manage the investment themselves or pay someone to do so.
- It is an investment capable of enhancement by pro-active management while there is nothing the individual can do to enhance their British Telecom shares – except make more phone calls!
- Property is not a standardised investment and information in the property market is imperfect. Moreover, confidentiality clauses are used by landlords to suppress information that may have an adverse effect on their property.
- There is no single market for commercial property.
- While the physical structure of the buildings is subject to obsolescence and will eventually require refurbishment or replacement, the land on which is stands is not generally a wasting asset.
- Property investment may come in a variety of legal titles, eg freehold, leasehold, under-leasehold.
- It is a growth investment. Investing for growth implies that the investor will be content with a low-income return from the property today in the expectation of increasing income and capital values in the future. Peculiarly the income does not rise as a steady progression, but rather in steps when rent reviews take place and when leases end or tenants vacate.
- Like virtually all investments, property is subject to risk. This risk

is least in prime sectors of the market and increases through the secondary market into the tertiary market. The income return or yield on property also rises as the risk increases or alternatively as the quality of the investment declines.

5.2 Value

The valuation of property assets is more art than science. It is a snap-shot in time approach heavily slanted towards the valuer's subjective view, built upon not only his firm's market experience of the category of property under consideration, but also by his interpretation of how this untargetted information should be applied to the property under valuation.

The phrase "value" can be highly emotive and is subject to a wide variety of interpretation. However, the definition generally accepted is that contained in the *Statements of Asset Valuation Practice and Guidance Notes* (colloquially known as the Red Book) issued by the Royal Institution of Chartered Surveyors.

Indeed the definition of open market value lies at the heart of the Red Book and it is now mandatory to comply with the Red Book for virtually all valuations which the general public at large may place reliance upon; ie stock exchange, annual accounts and financial reporting and valuations, which may be published and relied upon by people other than those to whom they are addressed.

However, it does not strictly apply to valuations for mortgages or loans secured on commercial property for the private purposes of the lender, albeit many lending sources stipulate a Red Book based valuation, since it is deemed to represent best practice.

Statement of Asset Valuation Practice number 2 defines open market value, in effect, as the best price at which the sale of an interest in property might reasonably be expected to have been completed unconditionally for cash consideration on the date of valuation, assuming:

- That there is a willing seller.
- That prior to the date of valuation there had been a reasonable period (having regard to the nature of the property and the state of the market) for the proper marketing of the interest, for the agreement of price and terms and for the completion of sale.
- That the state of the market, level of values and other circumstances were, on any earlier assumed date of exchange of contracts, the same as on the date of valuation.
- That no account is taken of any additional bid by a purchaser with a special interest.

5.3   Sectors of the market

We have already mentioned that property investment broadly falls into three categories being prime, secondary and tertiary. Conventional property wisdom states that the three main considerations are location, location and location. While this still holds good in part, the decline in the property market of the early 1990s widened the rent differential between well-specified and the under-specified buildings and those poorly located. In a weak market the take-up of space polarises towards the higher-specified and better-located properties.

By contrast in a strong market such as the boom of the late 1980s, the collective optimism that commercial rental growth would continue almost indefinitely led to a widening of the definition of prime and a general willingness by institutional investors to accept properties with "warts" that in a weak market would not be contemplated for institutional purchase.

As well as critically examining location, other factors of supreme importance are now cash flow, covenant and duration of income.

5.4   Cash flow

During the 1980s the use of a equivalent yields was the accepted measure of investment worth. The equivalent yield is one yield applied to both present income and expected reversion (based on current market rental levels). Thus a factory investment of 5,000 sq ft producing £15,000 pa with the review in two years and which has an open market rental value of £25,000 would have been valued thus:

		£
Current income	15,000	
Years' purchase in perpetuity		
at 10% (equivalent yield)	10	
		150,000
Increase upon reversion		
in two years	10,000	
Years' purchase of a reversion		
to perpetuity in two years @ 10%	8.264	
		82,640
		232,640
Thus the income profile would be:		
Initial yield	6.4%	
Reversionary yield	10.8%	

While an initial yield of 6% may have been acceptable in the 1980s boom, it most certainly has not been in the recession of the early 1990s. Investors will not accept a deficit finance situation whereby they have to pay part of the interest on borrowings out of their own pocket. To overcome this, the market measure of investment worth has become the initial yield and little weight is attached to rental uplifts on reversion especially if these are more than a couple of years remote.

If our example property above is revalued on an initial yield basis at say 10% the value becomes:

		£	
Current income		15,000	
Years purchase in perpetuity at 10%		10	
	Capital Value		£150,000

Thus investment value is now partly driven by immediate cash flow, but having secured a satisfactory volume of cash flow an investor then critically examines the quality or reliability of that cash flow, in other words the covenant strength.

In an extremely bearish market, investors considering the purchase of vacant properties will assume a significant void period of no rental income while tenants are found and also until rent begins to flow after the likely rent-free periods or incentives that will be used to attract the ingoing tenant to this property. This double void might typically be two years, which if looking at a 10% investment (10 years' purchase) will reduce it to just over eight years' purchase or discount the value by almost 20%.

Similar treatment is applied to properties with lease expiries or break clauses since the investor will assume the worst-case scenario, that rent will cease to flow for a period after the expiry/break and this results in a significant reduction in value.

5.5 Covenant
Location is still important, but in the 1990s the covenant – the standing of the tenant and their ability to go on paying the rent – has acquired far greater significance. In the short term at least property investment has become less about property and more about latching on to the cash flow of a strong company.

Purchasers are now focusing on the quality of the covenant; if the covenant is first class there will be competition among prospective purchasers because the continuity of income is virtually guaranteed. With a weak tenant who is more susceptible to defaulting on the rent, the building might even be unsaleable.

5.6 Duration

Leases that expire within 10 years or have a tenant's option to break are a major disincentive to investors and not only is it far more difficult to attract a purchaser, but any purchase will be at a subdued level.

Many lenders will only advance mortgages against investment properties where the tenant is tied in for 10 to 15 years or more. This puts properties with earlier lease expiries or breaks outside the market for those investors reliant upon borrowed money. Institutional investors applying their own funds can afford to be very choosey and they will not usually buy properties in this category (except at a discounted price). The net result is that the number of potential purchasers for this type of property is extremely limited, thus driving down the market price. It is a buyers market.

5.7 The shortening lease

One of the greatest and possibly longer term implications of the collapse in the commercial property market of the early 1990s has been the undermining of the structure of the "institutional lease"; the chassis upon which the commercial property vehicle has been constructed.

Under the 25-year institutional lease, the investor benefitted from:

- The undertaking by the tenant to pay for 25 years a rent that would never fall below the starting level (in reality it was expected to increase every five years).
- The security offered by the property itself and the relatively straightforward prospect of reletting the property if the existing tenant failed.

The early 1990s phenomenon of falling rents and over-rented buildings is a newcomer to the UK property market that has had lasting consequences:

- Where tenants are lost, landlords know that they will have problems replacing them even in a good-quality or prime building and they probably face a cut in the rent.
- If a landlord can keep his tenant and maintain his income, rental-growth prospects for the foreseeable future are negligible.

- Tenants face problems if they want to vacate existing buildings and assign the lease to somebody else. Quite frequently they have to pay the ingoing tenant a reverse premium in return for accepting liability for paying a rent over and above the market rate.
- Due to privity of contract, an assignor is still liable for the rent if the assignee defaults. This risk had always existed, but traditionally it was assumed that the building could be relet at the same or a better rent if the assignee defaulted. With an over-supply of space and declining rents, this risk became a real liability.

As a result prospective tenants sensing that the strength of their bargaining position has increased are challenging the traditional institutional lease structure. They will not commit themselves for 25 years preferring short-term leases of as little as 10 or even five years, possibly with a break clause. Lease terms are becoming more flexible with early break clauses being readily available and shorter lease terms being granted bringing UK leasing practice closer to American and European practice.

The other bastion of the institutional lease, the upwards-only rent review clause is equally under challenge.

Investors in the UK property market are averse to losing the certainty of a guaranteed long-term income, with the opportunity to take advantage of rising markets but fully insulated against falling rental markets. The result of these changes will certainly be an overall decline in the capital value of investment property.

Over-rented properties are being traded on the basis of initial yield combined with strength of covenant and length of lease. Hence such investments yields are much the same as long-dated guilts.

It is important for landlords to appreciate that it may be difficult to retrace steps in the future towards a 25-year fully-repairing and insuring lease once the traditional haven has been left. A tenant renewing under the Landlord and Tenant Act 1954 will expect concessionary terms in any renewal. The onus is on any party seeking renewal terms substantially different from the existing lease to justify the departure. Most reported cases are instances where the courts have considered the case for a change was not made out.

Landlords who wish to preserve their negotiating stength in the future, on the assumption that market conditions will by then have improved, should try to ensure that any lease which falls short of the former model "clear" 25-year fully-repairing and insuring lease, is contracted out of the 1954 Act, and consequently not entitled to renewal on the same terms.

CHAPTER 6

Rent collection and service charge

6.1 Rent collection

The two fundamental principles of rent collection are correctness of information and timing.

It is always good practice to demand rent, regardless of whether rent has to be legally demanded. In good times tenants will in the main pay rent promptly and in bad times they will look for an excuse to use the landlords credit for their own purpose. Invariably, tenants like to have something against which they can make payment whether it be a proforma application or a VAT invoice. Also, evidence of issued rent demands can prove invaluable in litigeous situations.

6.2 Information

Whenever records are being set up adequate details must be obtained from the tenant. It is of great assistance in rent collection for the landlord to ensure that he has the right address, that the demands are correctly set up in terms of periodic accounting with the right amounts (including relevant rate of VAT), and most importantly, a contact in the event that credit-control procedures (see below) are necessary. These records can be obtained from lease extracts and perhaps simpler, by making contact with the tenant itself. Routine circulars by way of a proforma questionnaire annexed to demands will ensure that the tenant's addresses, contact numbers and other information can be updated.

6.3 Demand format

A rent demand which sets out clearly and concisely the relevant element of the demand whether it be rent, service charge, insurance or sundries is a great assistance, as is the period to which it refers. For example, a demand stating "rent due June quarter" does not indicate whether the rent is due either in arrears or in advance.

A far more helpful approach would be "rent due – 24/6/93 – 28/9/93". Details of the net amount, VAT element and total is of assistance to the tenant just as are the relevant sections as to where the money should be paid and to whom. A good computer/data base system is more than capable of meeting these requirements.

6.4   Regularity

Many tenants operate a ledger system for processing rent. While some education may be necessary to advise that the rent demand/invoice is notification of the sum due, one can perhaps understand the problem which landlords instigate against themselves if they send out a demand, by way of tax invoice, a few days before the due date. Some tenants may feel that they are entitled to 30 days grace, which probably puts them unwittingly in breach. On the assumption that one tends to deal with traditional quarter days (March 25, June 24, September 29 and December 25 in each year) it is of benefit to send out the application/invoice by no later than the first week of the month in which the sum falls due in order that the tenants can post the relevant amount and ensure it is paid.

This is not normally a problem when dealing with large organisations such as national multiple retailers and Government bodies, who will invariably "programme" their systems so that rent is paid on or before the due date whether demanded or not. Indeed, it is pertinent that on some occasions the larger bodies are slower in instigating procedures to update their records for rent review purposes as invariably approval will need to be sought from senior managers, who may be instrumental in negotiating the increases.

6.5   Rent collection

Rent should be processed quickly. Money received should be batched and applied against the relevant period and amounts for which they are tendered. Many problems arise through tenants not giving an indication as to what the moneys they are paying are for. These are manifest where demands cover multiple items, eg rent, service charge, insurance and sundries (some of which items may have fallen due during the preceding quarter and which are being carried forward as arrears). There may need therefore to be some telepathy or indeed lateral thinking on the part of the landlord's accountant/managing agent and this is where the record systems as above will prove invaluable allowing the landlord's agent through good procedures to make contact with the relevant person in the tenant's purchase ledger/accounts department to ensure that the monies are correctly applied.

One should also be aware of the problem of tenants sending money to one agent covering a multiplicity of sites. Usually in such circumstances the tenant will send through a listing of the relevant properties which therefore provides an easy allocation.

It is vitally important that landlords and their agents understand that the time taken to get a posting right first time around is far more efficient than having to "unscramble" a posting which they think is right at the time and which will only manifest itself possibly some days or weeks later when stringent credit control procedures are applied.

6.6 Follow up

Effective rental collection is very much a barometer of the tenant's ability to pay and thus its trading position. Leaving aside those who make a payment well before or on the due quarter day, there are some parties who invariably take one or two days to respond.

Dependant on the clients attitude and the terms of the lease by which one, two or even 21-days grace may actually be allowable before penalty interest applies, one has to evaluate rent collection, often objectively and in many cases, subjectively. It is important however to understand that within a short period of time after the due quarter day the demand should be followed up.

The methods of reminder are individual depending on the landlord's/managing agent's policies however, it may take the form of a final red reminder after say five days, a written warning of impending action after 10 and a final warning after 15/21 days. None of these time-limits are offered as suggestions, merely to impress upon the reader the importance of follow-up.

It is possible after a period of time in managing a particular investment to ascertain the good and poor payers and who would be at risk. The importance of keeping records of payment dates by way of cash history can play a vital role in foreseeing warning signs and maybe relevant in credit control: see Chapter 8 for further discussion.

For example, a good payer by way of a business (possibly a private limited company), who misses a payment by three weeks could, if action is not taken early enough, be pre-empted by a notice from an administrative receiver and/or liquidator. It is also relevant that other parties may well be pursuing credit control at an earlier stage thus overriding the landlords position.

6.7   Tenants in breach

Just as it is important to demand rent promptly, there are occasions when it is wholly undesireable to demand money. Where there is a breach either implied or specific on a property, a landlord or its agent should be aware of the consequences of demanding and/or receiving rents which might waive the breach and prejudice the landlord's right to alternative remedies. The essence of good record keeping and appropriate systems to flag such breaches and ensure that demands are not posted or if they are or are not received is important.

6.8   Client accounting

Just as it is important to receive rents and other money, the correct application to either client accounts or expenditure (in the case of service charge) accounts is of relevance. Landlords do not generally welcome money remaining in managing agents' accounts when such funds could be put to beneficial use. On the basis that clients only approve retention of money pending general and periodic clearance, it is essential that the appropriate deposit and interest bearing accounts are set up with the full knowledge and agreement of the client. Transfer of money to the client should be accompanied by clear and defined statements identifying the money demanded, received and arrears carried forward.

By way of summary it is important that rent is demanded and processed quickly and that the tenants are educated as to the dates upon which they should make payment and that follow up procedures under the normal course of events are observed If any one thing antagonises landlords more in management, it is the inability of agents to collect rent promptly and efficiently.

6.9   Credit control

There will inevitably be times when formal credit control procedures are necessary and in this section a number of issues are addressed. In many cases a tenant's inability to pay will not be apparent. A late payment of one quarter does not always mean that it will be persistently late, for example, a computer system may have been modified, personnel and procedures may have changed, all of which could fall under the general category of "team or administrative problems".

6.10 Interest on late payment

Where leases provide for interest on late payment either after the requisite number of days or from the due date up until receipt, it is important and indeed recommended that landlords should seek to apply this by way of penalty. Even if after due analysis the landlord agrees to waive the interest, the fact that it has been considered, applied and negotiations have subsequently taken place, show that the landlord is in control.

6.11 Pre-emptive action

As part of the tenant-cash history, a record will be built up of tenants who are persistently late and it is therefore possible to invoice tenants who are regularly in breach earlier than the due date in order to "remind" them. As with all credit control procedures, records as to correspondence, conversations, names, times and dates are of vital importance if one is to prove the case at a later date.

6.12 Formal action

The general rule if one is going to take formal action is to "get in first". There are numerous bodies with powers either equal to or greater than landlords. These may include local authorities pursuing for statutory demands such as rates, suppliers including national utilities, HM Customs & Excise and others. Landlords with outstanding rent are generally unsecured creditors and in the event of the tenant being forced into liquidation, receivership or bankruptcy (in the case of an individual) the prospects of being paid are slight, particularly in times of recession: see the sections on tenant failure for a detailed discourse.

In more healthier climes, it may be possible to deal with an insolvency practitioner who can see there is a prospect of disposing of the lease for a premium, at which time the landlord can recover the arrears as part of the assignment.

The forms of action open to a landlord are various and it is not proposed to deal in any great detail in this section. Suffice it to say that use of solicitors to either issue warning letters or proceedings by way of writs will often have the desired affect. The most effective remedy is the use of certificated bailiffs to pursue the remedy of distress. This common law remedy for a commercial lease does not have the sanction of the court and has the advantage of being extremely effective in that not only is it often an unpleasant experience for the subject tenant, but that in most modern leases, all the costs are recoverable. The feeling of "distress" is often exactly what it causes to the tenant.

It should also be borne in mind that by using certificated bailiffs, their knowledge of insolvency law will result in a far greater success than negotiating directly with the tenant. They are able to secure an advantage where third-party receivers or insolvency practitioners are involved. Before carrying out such an action it is essential that one's client is fully briefed as to the situation, has sanctioned the specific action and once bailiffs are instructed, all parties on the landlord's side should endeavour to negotiate through the bailiff rather than become involved in direct contact. Experience has shown that where landlords or agents agree to negotiate after instructing bailiffs, the chances of success in debt recovery are substantially diminished.

6.13 Forfeiture
The opportunities presented to the landlord in terms of asset management by means of credit control should not be overlooked: see below under "The remedy of forfeiture" for further discussion of this remedy.

In summary, this section highlights the need for landlords to be very clear on the form of credit control they wish to apply, the procedures and the authorities which they will need to have in place before implementing such a course of action and the resolve to pursue it through to the end.

A final point however must be the relevance of pursuing a bad debt; it is completely futile to pursue a debt where there is no possibility of ultimate success. Although it may be tempting to pursue a debtor to the final degree, unless there are specific reasons it may well be more positive to cut ones losses and withdraw from lengthy proceedings which may well result in adverse publicity and tarnish the reputation of all parties concerned.

6.14 The service charge
Operation of the service charge is exclusively governed by the form of lease adopted and accordingly the first point of reference must be the lease.

The single objective of a service charge is to enable the landlord to recover all likely anticipated expenditure not only for the property in its present form, but envisaging any reasonable extension or alteration in the future. Service charge clauses in leases should ideally be identical in every lease in a block of property so that the block can be managed efficiently and is regarded as a "clean investment". The recovery provisions should add up to 100%.

The service charge for any property can be apportioned by reference to:

1. specified floor areas (or a floor-area formula)
2. rateable value
3. specific percentages.

Apportionment based on floor areas is preferable. Rateable value apportionment can be subject to inequities and is no longer in common use. Fixed percentages, while they give certainty and generally avoid dispute, become unworkable if, for example, the property is enlarged or part of the property is upgraded.

Large shopping centres for example may include a weighted floor area formula whereby a discount is given for large space occupiers.

When administering services charges on behalf of a client (ie acting as managing agent) the property manager must comply with the RICS Members Accounts Regulations. It is also good practice to obtain an independent year-end audit from independent chartered accountants.

Some leases provide for the landlord to supply tenants with a formal service-charge estimate at the commencement of the service-charge year. When budgeting, account should be taken of anticipated inflationary increases and also items of extraordinary expenditure such as refurbishment work and the replacement of major plant. Further adjustments may need to be made where, for example, the VAT status of the property has changed during the year.

Initial issues

What the service charge covers depends on the services to be provided by the landlord, the condition of the building and the type of tenants in occupation.

These are the initial key points:

- Whether to use a mechanism involving fixed percentages.
- Whether to use a mechanism based on a proportion fixed by an independent surveyor in the event of dispute.
- Whether to use a mechanism involving floor areas or some other basis of allocation.

What the landlord has to do
The tenant will want to make the landlord provide the services that are vital to his use of the property and his business, such as the repair of the structure of the property and of the common parts.

The landlord will only want to do what can be claimed from the tenant in the service charge. This means reserving a right not to provide the services in certain circumstances and an exclusion of liability for anything that happens beyond his control.

What the tenant has to pay for
The landlord will want the tenant to pay for as many of the services as possible, but he should consider the following:

• The need for consistency between different leases in the same building.
• The need to identify specific expenditure to be reclaimed.
• The need for general clauses in the service charge provisions of the lease to pick up future services.

If the property has different users, the lease should distinguish between different types of expenditure and the class of tenant by whom it is payable in the service charge.

How the service charge is arrived at
The tenant's share of the service charge can be determined by percentage or by proportion.

A percentage basis usually relates to floor areas or rateable values at completion of the lease. This avoids future arguments, but is fixed for the term of the lease. The landlord may want the right to change the percentage later if the circumstances of the lease change.

A proportion basis usually relates to the proportion which the floor area of the premises bears to the floor areas of all the other premises in the property; or on a similar basis by reference to the rateable value of the premises against that of all the other premises in the property.

The problem with the proportion basis is agreeing the right method of measuring floor areas.

The next issue is the collection of the service charge from the tenant. The lease will have to deal with how the service charge is calculated, certified and what happens in the event of a dispute. It must also cover payment in advance and accounting at the year end.

6.15 Management companies

Apart from blocks of flats, the principal use of management companies, is in business parks and mixed-use developments where there are likely to be a multiplicity of users, ownership and tenure. The objective of the management company is to integrate these diverse interests to enable the development to be managed in its entirety to the benefit of all with an interest in both the long and short term.

The responsibilities of the management company will be set out in the memorandum and articles of association of the company which should include the following:

1. To provide and carry out the necessary services for the management of the development in the interest of good estate management efficiently and cost effectively.
2. To appoint a board of directors and company secretary.
3. To hold an annual general meeting.
4. To produce audited service charge accounts.
5. To make an annual return to Companies House.

The freeholder/developer may wish to maintain overall control of the company during the development process to ensure uniform standards of design and maintenance. On completion of the development he may no longer have an interest in safeguarding the design and maintenance and provision should be made for the surrender of his shares to the management company.

Shares are generally issued by reference to site acreage or floor area. They normally vest with the owner of the principal (or most valuable) interest in that part of the development, ie the freeholder or long leaseholder, but rarely the tenant in occupation on a rack-rented lease.

From the property manager's stance, the most effective disposal is on a long-leasehold basis since the usual covenants and service charge provisions are incorporated in the lease and are enforceable against the existing and subsequent lessees. The disadvantage is that this may damage the investment value and freehold sales are often preferred.

In the event of a freehold sale being negotiated, it should be subject to a deed of covenant whereby the purchaser will contribute to the service charge. There is, however, doubt as to whether such positive covenants are enforceable against subsequent owners and hence future management problems can be created.

CHAPTER 7

Warning signs and problem areas

There are signs which warn the landlord and its managing agent of problem areas and tenant failure.

The issue is what to look for.

The basic rule for the landlord and his managing agent is to get to know thoroughly and see your tenant early and often. It would be inadequate management to make an investigation on the grant of the lease and then fail to keep a regular check on how the tenant's business is progressing.

7.1 What to look for

While tenant failure and subsequent insolvency arises as often as not because of a shortage of money, this is a position which invariably takes place after a business has suffered a period of deterioration due to bad management.

At the outset before a new lease is granted and while it is running the nature of the tenant's business has to be assessed in commercial terms. This is quite separate from the need to assess a tenant's business in environmental and estate management terms, which is dealt with elsewhere.

Here are some issues to consider:

- Whether the tenant's business is a new venture. A business with an existing good track record speaks for itself. A business which has recently moved into an unfamiliar market may be suspect especially where the shift in market is designed to replace a fall in its existing range of products.
- Whether there is likely to be a decline in the demand for the services or the product of the tenant's existing market.
- Whether the market in which the tenant's business currently operates is likely to be eroded by foreign imports, exchange values, or overseas competition on exports.
- Whether the tenant's business is dependent upon a sole trader or key-man or any particular class or type of customer or supplier or the tenant operates in a market where a failure or receivership in

any of its customers or suppliers (and indeed creditors) is likely to have a knock-on effect. This happens, for example, in the construction business where a receivership of the developer usually signals bankruptcy for the individual trade subcontractors.
- Whether the tenant's business is part of a large group, but new to the area in which it is taking a lease. A tenant starting up a satellite operation in a new location may be subject to controls and procedure from head office which make communication difficult between landlord and tenant or may lead from poor managerial control to business failure.
- Whether simple inspection of the premises reveals a lack of managerial control, eg in stock levels, empty offices or idle staff.

The audited accounts of the tenant's business also need to be considered:

- *The date*: whether the accounts are the most recent.
- Whether there are any management accounts to bring the position up to date.
- *Stock*: the basis on which stock is controlled and how this is reflected in the accounts.
- *Auditor's certificate*: this usually tells little, but any qualified certificate should ring alarm bells immediately.
- Liquidity ratios: look at the relationship between current assets and liabilities and how the cash flow is structured. This will be particularly clear if the business appears to be dependent upon borrowing in the short term to meet immediate cash-flow problems. This also may evidence a lack of management control or cash flow.

It would also be useful to know whether any of the secured creditors have the benefit of guarantees from the owners which itself shows the extent to which the owners of the business are committed to it and what alternative security there may be available to the landlord.

7.2 Warning signs
If the landlord and his managing agent know the tenant then they will be able to identify when they are receiving an excuse or a genuine reason for late payment of rent.

However, these are some of the warning signs:

- Where the tenant makes a partial payment of rent with the promise to pay the balance shortly.
- Where the tenant makes no payment at all, but maintains that it

will be paid in full shortly.
- Where the tenant pays the rent, but refuses to pay the insurance premium or the service charge because of an outstanding issue with the landlord.
- Where the tenant refuses to pay the rent and takes issue with the terms of the rent demand or invoice.
- Where the tenant refuses to pay the rent on the basis of the landlords failure to comply with its obligations under the lease either as to the services to be provided or the repair of common parts.

There are also a number of early-warning signs apparent to a landlord or managing agent that regularly inspects property and gets to know the tenant well:

- Where there are constant changes or reduction in staff.
- Where there is an increasing amount of old or idle stock around the premises or a build up of finished products.
- Where the use of the premises changes or a new use is started up in conjunction with the existing use both without landlord's prior consent.
- Where the tenant sublets part of the premises or shares occupation with another party without obtaining the landlord's consent.
- Where key persons in the tenant's business are either unavailable or no longer working at the premises.

In all these cases prompt action is necessary to protect the landlord's interest in the premises. This is dealt with in the earlier Chapter 6 on rent collection.

CHAPTER 8

Short-term solutions

In weak or poor market conditions, landlords need to retain flexibility of approach and be prepared to offer incentive packages to attract the right calibre of tenant. The right tenant will not only provide a reliable or bankable income stream, but also enhance the capital value of the investment. In a market where businesses are contracting and averse to making new property commitments, any tenant may be the "right" tenant and may well need seducing into making a significant commitment to the property.

The section below deals with the features of a poor market which evolves in response to paucity of tenant demand, oversupply of competing building stock and the increasing bargaining strength of the tenant in such a market. The matters to be considered are:

- lease duration
- upwards-only rent review
- clear leases
- privity of contract
- rent-free periods
- cash incentives
- confidentiality clauses

8.1   Lease duration

The property market in the UK relies on long-term funding from the investment institutions – insurance companies in particular – and increasingly private money from overseas buyers. One of its main attractions is the unique security of income provided by the traditional UK lease structure, allowing the investor to match property assets against long-term liabilities.

In a poor market the forces of supply and demand have effect and prospective tenants, with the upper hand, demand shorter leases or less onerous terms. The result is the creation of a two tier market: new lettings and shorter-term leases being dominated by market forces, while the bulk of the market is made up of existing leases negotiated in better market conditions for longer (probably

25-year) terms.

It is likely given the cyclical nature of the property market, that when the peak in the property cycle returns the landlord is again dominant and the roles are reversed and market forces at that time allow the landlord to dictate the terms on which he will do business.

Shorter leases do not find favour with investors, who prefer locking in the tenant's covenant and not having to worry about the property for considerable periods of time. To tempt institutions to buy with shorter leases, sellers may have to discount the price in compensation for the future uncertainty.

Similarly, any property company or private investor, reliant upon borrowed finance finds that banks and other lenders are averse to taking properties with much less than 15 years unexpired on the lease as security for a loan.

8.2   Upwards-only rent reviews

Upwards-only rent reviews are one of the key features of institutionally acceptable leases in the United Kingdom. They effectively give landlords the opportunity to take advantage of rising rental market trends, but offer a full indemnity against any decline in market rental trends.

Landlords jealously guard upwards-only rent reviews to ensure that the lease created is to an institutionally acceptable standard.

The upwards-only rent review is of paramount importance in a market characterised by over-rented situations. By way of example, office accommodation let in a good market may in a poor market be worth not much more than 50% of the rent secured under the lease. This creates what is commonly known as an over-rented building. Although the growth prospect for such properties are remote, investors are still prepared to buy the income stream, but if the tenants fail, their likely income stream might halve. This is why covenant strength is paramount in these circumstances.

If the hypothetical over-rented property did not benefit from an upwards-only rent review, the value of the investment would be significantly depleted, if, for example it exposed the landlord to a large reduction in income. The message here is that landlords should hold out for upwards only reviews even to the extent of trading alternative concessions against the tenant's desire to secure an upwards/downwards rent review opportunity.

8.3 Clear leases

An investor's objective is normally to maximise the income stream received from and the capital value of any given property. The income stream must be a "spendable" income free of all deduction.

Landlords should therefore seek to impose all maintenance, repairing, rates liabilities and other outgoings upon the building occupier. This can be done either by a direct covenant or, in a multi-occupied building, by means of a service charge. This is discussed further in para 6.14.

Landlords should resist tenants seeking anything less than a full repairing obligation. Where this is impossible due either to the weakness of the market or more particularly the condition of the building, then a full repairing obligation, limited by a schedule of condition taken at the commencement of the lease may be a compromise acceptable to both parties.

Leases limiting repairing obligation by reference to a schedule of condition or which impose internal repairing obligations only and leave both the responsibility and cost of external and structural maintenance with the landlord are not acceptable to institutional purchasers nor to most property companies. A "defective" repairing covenant will most certainly lead to a diminution in the value of the investment property.

8.4 Privity of contract

Property investors, under the present doctrine of privity of contract, are, in the event of tenant default on rent or other terms of the lease, able to pursue the original tenant. Chapters 3 and 19 deal more fully with the legal aspects of privity of contract.

The logic underlying the privity rule is that a lease is an agreement freely entered into by the landlord and tenant; no tenant has to sign if they do not wish to. If they do sign a lease for say, 25 years, they should be prepared to accept responsibility for those 25 years. It is not for the law to interfere with contracts freely entered into in the open market.

This doctrine is under close scrutiny because it has worked unfairly particularly against, for example, individual sole traders who have sold their business and leasehold premises and retired only to be faced many years later with the rent and repairing obligations that they felt had long since been left behind. According to those who oppose change, if the privity of contract doctrine were abolished, landlords would simply become unwilling to agree to lease assignments or subletting.

The privity rule has been a further safety net to investors and is of crucial importance during difficult market conditions. This is for at least two reasons:

- The greater risk of the occupying tenant business failing in a recession.
- The greater difficulty of letting older and secondary buildings in a climate of little tenant demand. With state of the art, quality or prime buildings new tenants are more easily found and therefore the income stream can be quickly reinstated from an alternative tenant. It may however not be reinstated at the previous level if that rent had been fixed in strong market conditions: see para 8.2).

8.5   Rent-free periods

Rent-free periods are a long-established feature of the UK property market. Their traditional place was typically in the letting of units in a shopping centre to enable the trader to fit the unit out to their own house style with rent commencement coinciding with the beginning of trading. These would typically be for periods of six weeks or three months.

Given the greater bargaining power of tenants, landlords have quickly identified rent-free periods as a relatively inexpensive concession to offer to the tenant (without significant damage to its reversionary interest).

Rather than give concessions on length of term, upward only rent reviews, repairing obligations or privity of contract it is often preferable for a landlord to trade-off rent income.

It is usually preferable for the landlord to give this rent discount by way of a rent-free period rather than a reduction on the rent roll throughout the five years to the first review. Thus for example a rent-free period of one year is in simple terms the equivalent of a 20% annual discount on rent assuming a five-yearly rent review pattern. By preserving the "headline rent" the investor derives two significant benefits:

- The rental evidence created is (in our example 20%) higher than it might have been which must be helpful for rent review purposes on similar or adjoining properties.
- Investment property purchasers are buying the income stream and capital values are calculated by applying a multiplier to the

actual rent income. It is much better to apply such a multiplier to 100% of the income rather than to 80% of the income, even if it does mean that the landlord has to wait for 12 months before he has an income producing and therefore saleable investment. However, even this can be overcome by the landlord himself making up the rent in the first year for the purchaser, so as to protect the purchaser's clear income stream from day one.

It would be unfair to leave the reader with the impression that rent-free periods are exclusively a device used by landlords to maintain the value of their investment. There are plentiful examples of landlords granting leases, sometimes of fairly short duration with say no rent whatsoever in the first three years and a break clause at year three. Illogical though this may seem, it does show the extremes to which some landlords, particularly those with secondary property in areas of gross over supply, have had to go, fundamentally so as not to have to pay the rates liability or fund the service-charge costs themselves. For further discussion on the liability to rates see below under "The Empty Property".

8.6 Cash incentives
A further elaboration on the rent-free period is some form of incentive paid to the tenant "up front". Usually this takes the form of a cash payment which might euphemistically be labelled as a landlord's contribution to the tenant's fitting-out costs.

The sole objective of any such side deal is to leave the headline rent undented and, in so far as it is possible, unquestioned. Landlords have become extremely inventive with the incentives packages that tenants are being given.

8.7 Confidentiality clauses
Having created an artificial "headline rent" by propping it up with rent-free periods or other tenant incentives, landlords do their level best to conceal the matters from other operators within the property market. If, for example, rent review surveyors uncover all of the facts of the deal they will analyse those other elements to reduce the headline rent to the "underlying rent". This obviously has an undesireable affect on the outcome, at least from the landlords stance, on any subsequent rent reviews and most certainly does not enhance the value of their investment.

The most popular means of seeking to supress such pertinent

information has been the confidentiality clause. However, it is difficult to enforce. Moreover, since the life blood of the property market is information, and surveyors are extremely adept at ferreting out what they need to know, as often as not the "confidential" parts of a transaction are common knowledge within the market.

CHAPTER 9

Rent review

The main purpose of a rent review clause is to protect a landlord's spendable-income stream from the effects of inflation on property values. Without a rent review clause, what may have started out as a fair rent in the first year, may, within a few years, become a completely uneconomic rent because property values have risen in the meantime.

A way round this problem would be to grant only short-term leases. However, the disadvantage is uncertainty: uncertainty whether the landlord will in fact be able to relet in the open market at a proper rent within a short period of time; and uncertainty whether the tenant will be able (at the end of his short term lease) to outbid any competing potential tenants to continue his occupation of the premises.

The rent review clause attempts to provide an alternative to reletting the premises every few years by, importing a hypothetical rather than a real reletting.

The typical five-yearly review of rent is probably the most important benchmark in the property cycle giving the investor a chance to enjoy the uplift in income which justifies his decision to invest at an initial yield often lower than can be obtained from alternative investment media. However, where properties are already "over-rented" rent reviews will not produce a higher rent.

On the positive side, the landlord is likely to be protected against reduced income under the terms of the lease and in part is therefore insulated from volatile market rental value trends. This must be viewed again the reliance placed on the tenant's covenant; if the tenant fails there will be a substantial loss of income while a reletting is secured and a diminution in the income afterwards.

Lease terms are becoming more flexible with early break clauses being easily available and shorter-lease terms being granted; bringing UK leasing practice closer to American and European laws.

Over-rented properties are being traded on the basis of initial yield combined with strength of covenant and length of lease. Hence such investments yield much the same as long-dated guilts. Provided the income is secure and tenant default is unlikely, investing on this basis is safe and akin to investing in a guaranteed income-producing asset and in such cases the income is guaranteed until the end of the lease.

The rent review clause usually allows, in the first instance, the parties themselves to agree what rent might be expected to be payable if the premises were relet on the rent review date under a similar form of lease to that already granted. If the parties cannot reach agreement, there is usually provision for one or other of them to apply for the appointment of a valuer to fix a rent at a level he believes the premises might reasonably obtain in the open market (in rent review parlance often referred to as "the open market rental value").

Because the landlord is not actually reletting the premises in the open market, and because the rent review provisions are being exercised against the background that the tenant is in actual fact continuing to occupy the premises under the terms of his existing lease, most rent review clauses will set out various assumptions to be made and various matters to be disregarded (which are often referred to simply as "disregards").

Over recent years the courts have gone out of their way to construe the language used in rent review clauses to produce the most sensible and realistic commercial result. In *British Gas Corporation* v *Universities Superannuation Scheme Ltd* [1986] 1 EGLR 120 it was held that unless there are clear and explicit provisions to the contrary the parties are to be taken as having intended that the hypothetical tenancy is on the same terms (other than as to *quantum* of rent) as those still subsisting between the parties in the actual existing lease, because that would give effect to the general intention underlying the incorporation of a rent review clause. This evolution has been christened the "presumption of reality".

The most obvious assumption is that the hypothetical letting is to be broadly on the terms of the actual lease (indeed this is such an obvious assumption that it will be implied in absence of words to the contrary). Another fundamental disregard is to disregard the tenant's continued occupation so that a valuer cannot take into account the fact that the actual tenant might well be willing to pay a rent above the open market rental value so as to safeguard his continued occupation.

Different assumptions and disregards may be needed in different circumstances. For example, a lease of a piece of land on which a tenant (at his own expense) constructs a building, may contain provisions in the rent review clause either to assume that no building has been built or to disregard the existence of the building actually built. The intended effect of such an assumption or disregard would be to allow the landlord to recover merely increases in the value of the land and not increases in the value of the building constructed on that land.

As will also be seen from this example, the same intention may often be expressed either as an assumption (that no building has been built) or as a disregard (of the fact that the building has in fact been built).

9.1   Matters typically dealt with in "Assumptions" and "Disregards"

These fall into the following categories:
- terms of existing lease
- hypothetical term
- goodwill
- letting as a whole
- vacant possession
- performance of consents
- improvements
- market incentives

A practical example of how the provisions of a lease are interpreted is shown in *London & Leeds Estates Ltd* v *Paribas Ltd* [1993] 2 EGLR 149.

Terms of the existing lease
In the absence of an express direction to the contrary, it is automatically assumed that a rent review will be on the basis of the terms of the existing lease with such alterations only as are expressly directed: as authority for this proposition see for instance *Basingstoke and Deane Borough Council* v *Host Group Ltd* [1987] 2 EGLR 147.

Since the primary purpose of the rent review clause is to reflect increases in the open market rental value of the premises let under the terms of the actual lease, any assumption of different lease terms or the disregard of the existing lease terms should be looked at carefully. The one lease term that is usually (and quite rightly) expressly disregarded is the amount of the rent actually being paid under the lease prior to the date of the review. Without this disregard there is at least an argument that the new open market rental value for the premises may, for instance, be reduced if the new open market rental value would represent a *quantum* leap from the rent previously payable. To go beyond this limited disregard of the terms of the existing lease there is a danger that the parties may end up valuing a hypothetical letting on entirely different terms to the existing lease, thereby defeating the underlying purpose of the rent review clause.

Note that any onerous or potentially onerous clauses in the original lease (such as an obligation on the tenant not merely to keep premises in repair, but also, if need be, to completely rebuild them) will have a potentially depressive effect on the open market rental value: the argument is simply that, in the open market, one would expect a potential tenant to offer a lower rent for premises being let on onerous terms than for the same or similar premises let on less onerous terms.

Length of the hypothetical term

Without any express assumptions to the contrary, at each rent review date the open market rental value for the premises would be set having regard to the unexpired residue of the term of years granted by the original lease. Thus, at a rent review in the 20th year of a 25-year lease, one would have regard to a term of five years, being all that remained of the original term of years at that date.

All things being equal, this is likely to depress the rent at the 20th-year review, following the reasoning that a potential tenant in the open market would give consideration to the fact that he might have to go to the trouble and expense of finding new premises in five years time.

However, because in practice the tenant will usually enjoy statutory rights to renew his tenancy under the provisions of Part II of the Landlord and Tenant Act 1954 it may be unfair to allow him to benefit from an assumption in year 20 that he has only a five-year term remaining when in fact he will usually have at least potential rights to renew his lease for a longer term. (The case of *Secretary of State for the Environment* v *Pivot Properties Ltd* (1980) 256 EG 1176 is authority for the proposition that it is entirely proper to consider the prospects of renewal).

By contrast, the assumption at every rent review date that the tenant has a full 25-year lease to run is likely to unfairly prejudice the tenant, who will not in fact enjoy such security of tenure. He may well have the prospect of renewing his lease under the 1954 Act, but he does not have any certainty that he will be able to do so: for example, the landlord may prevent the tenant renewing if the landlord intends to occupy the premises for a business carried on by himself or if he intends to redevelop the premises.

A compromise between the two alternatives (and one recommended in the Law Society model form of rent review clause) is an assumption that the hypothetical letting will be for a term equal to the unexpired residue of the actual lease or (in the case of a 25-year lease with a five yearly rent review pattern) a period of say 10 years, whichever is the longer.

Landlords wishing to impose an assumption of a term of years equal to the term originally granted at every rent review date (for instance an assumption that at each rent review date there are 25 years remaining) should note the recent case of *Lynnthorpe Enterprises Ltd* v *Sidney Smith (Chelsea) Ltd* [1990] 2 EGLR 131. Here the assumption of "a term of years equivalent to the said term" (ie the term granted by the original lease) was construed as meaning a term of years equivalent to the original term *but starting on the first day of the term*: in other words the unexpired residue of the original term of years and not (as the landlord had intended) a term equivalent to the original term starting afresh at each rent review date.

One must however proceed with caution since what has been accepted as a beneficial assumption for a landlord over the last 20 years is rapidly being overturned by recession. In times of economic and financial uncertainty the business planning cycle is shorter and there is an overwhelming argument that shorter lease terms are more marketable and hence more valuable than longer ones.

Goodwill attaching to the business carried on by the tenant or any permitted subtenant
This is invariably disregarded for similar reasons to the disregard of the tenant's occupation. Any goodwill attaching to the business carried on from the premises represents the value of the tenant's (or subtenant's) business and not the premises themselves. If the rent review clause contains no disregard of goodwill attaching to the business carried on from the premises, there is a danger to the tenant that his landlord will be able to argue for a higher open

market rent on the basis that a potential tenant in the same line of business as the tenant might be willing to pay a higher rent to secure these particular premises. If for instance once particular premises become well known as say, a supermarket, it is quite likely that another supermarket chain might be more interested in acquiring a lease of these particular premises so as to be able to trade on the fact that potential customers are aware of, and used to going to, the premises to purchase supermarket goods. The position is shown, for example, in *Prudential Assurance Co Ltd* v *Grand Metropolitan Estates Ltd* [1993] EGCS 58 where the disregard of occupation included the disregard of goodwill.

Letting of premises as a whole
In the absence of any express assumption that the premises are to be let either as a whole or in parts there will be an implied assumption that: (i) the premises are to be let as a whole; and (ii) on the terms of the particular lease, including any rights under that lease to sublet part.

Consider a rent review clause in a lease of a large multi-storey office block which contains no assumption either way as to a presumed letting of the whole or lettings in parts. Applying the implied assumptions, we would need to consider what rent single tenants in the open market would be willing to pay to take a lease of the whole building, whether for their own occupation or (if sublettings of parts are permitted under the terms of the actual lease of the premises) for subletting in parts at profitable sublease rents. So long as subletting is permitted under the terms of the particular lease and landlord's consent to any such sublettings is not to be unreasonably withheld, it is quite proper to consider what prospective tenants for the whole building might hope to recover in the way of sublease rents in the open market. The level of sublease rents they might expect to receive would (all things being equal) have a strong influence on how much rent they are willing to pay for a lease of the whole block and, most importantly, such tenants might be prepared to pay a higher rent for a lease of the whole than would other tenants who simply wanted to occupy the premises themselves with no ability to profitably subletting any parts of the block.

In considering what level of rent potential tenants might be willing to pay for a lease of the whole block if their intention was to sublet parts, regard will obviously be taken of the likely level of sublease rents that would be obtainable from sublettings of parts. However, from the aggregate of these sublease rents will need to be deducted.

- A reasonable risk reward for the potential head-tenant.
- Some element of "management charge" to compensate the head-tenant for the costs in administrative time of managing the building and collecting rents, providing services and the like.
- A rental "cushion" to protect against the risk of not being able to continuously sublet the various parts of the building at a profitable rent.

Contrast this position with a different rent review clause for a similar building which contains an express assumption that the open market rental shall be the higher of the rent obtained from either a letting of the premises as a whole or the aggregate of the rents obtained from sublettings of parts.

Such an assumption excludes from any valuation of the aggregate rents from sublettings of parts, the profit risk and management elements that would reduce this figure in the real open market and such an assumption can therefore work injustice on a tenant of the whole building who might find himself paying a rent that he would, in practice, be most unlikely to recoup from underlettings of the building in parts.

An express assumption that the building is to be let as a whole makes no practical difference to the situation where there is no such express assumption: namely one must assume (because it is an express assumption) a letting of the whole building to a single tenant assuming (unless there is any express assumption to the contrary) that the letting will be on the terms of the present lease.

Unusual frequency of review
In Chapter 5, we described the characteristics of property investment, one of the most important of which is it's growth prospects. This growth does not arrive as a steady stream, but rather in steps when rent reviews and reversions occur.

In general terms, landlords require reviews as frequently as possible and if they suffer infrequent reviews they will require compensation by way of an enhancement in the basic rental level in return for foregoing the opportunity of more frequent increases.

A further major problem is the paucity of evidence for unusual rent review patterns. If for example a lease was granted in 1972 for 42 years with one review only, in 1993, the probability is that in 1993 there will be no evidence of properties being let for periods of 21 years without review.

The problem is one of valuation, not of law. There are various theoretical methods which can be employed to convert rents from one review cycle to another. These basically hinge on a discounted cashflow technique.

Alternatively, there are a number of valuation tables, for example, *Bowcocks Property Valuation Tables*, *Donaldsons Investment Tables* or *Parrys Valuation and Investment Tables* which can be used to reduce a rent for a fixed term down to an annual equivalent rental value and then reconvert it back to another, but different, fixed-term rental.

In practice, these approaches tend to produce unpalatably high adjustments and the markets reaction has been to find a rule of thumb. This rule of thumb generally allocates a 1% addition for every year by which the review pattern exceeds the norm. Thus on a 21-year review pattern, where the rest of the market is operating on a five-year cycle, there would be a 16% addition to the basic rent drawn from comparables on a five-yearly cycle.

Letting of premises with vacant possession
Linked to the above assumption is the similar, and sometimes overlapping, assumption that the premises shall be assumed to be offered for letting with vacant possession, ie as empty premises.

Such an assumption does have the effect of requiring that any actual subleases must be ignored, but does not prevent the valuer taking account (if the terms of the lease permit subletting) of the potential to profitably sublet the premises in parts.

Conversely, where there is no express stipulation that the rent review is to be conducted on the assumption that the premises are available for letting with vacant possession, the case of *Forte & Co Ltd* v *General Accident Life Assurance Ltd* [1986] 2 EGLR 115 has held that the rents actually being paid under existing subleases can be taken into account.

Problems are only likely to arise where a tenant has arranged a particularly profitable subletting of part, over and above what would be expected in the open market. With an assumption of vacant possession the particular subletting is ignored; without the assumption, it may be taken into account with the possible risk that the tenant of the whole premises ends up paying a reviewed rent that is higher than would be expected in the open market. This is shown in *Laura Investment Co Ltd* v *Havering London Borough Council (No 2)* [1993] 08 EG 120.

Do not forget that even if an item is a fixture and therefore part of the premises, if it is a tenant's fixture it will not be taken into account on review if there is an assumption in the review clause that the premises are to be valued with vacant possession.

Performance of covenants

There will usually be an express assumption that the tenant has complied with its obligations under the lease. Less frequently, there is also an assumption that both landlord and tenant have complied with their respective obligations under the lease.

The argument in favour of an assumption that the tenant has complied with its obligations is clearly intended to prevent a tenant profiting from his own wrong by, for instance, failing to carry out its repairing obligations so that the premises end up in a shabby condition with the result that the open market rental value for the premises is reduced. With the assumption that the tenant *has* complied with its obligations under the lease, even if the premises are virtually falling down because the tenant has neglected its repairing obligations, the landlord can nevertheless in theory recover the open market rent that would be payable assuming that the tenant had repaired the premises. It would be unfair for a tenant to fail to carry out repairs and benefit by paying a lower rent as a result. In practice it is difficult to divorce the arbitrator's or expert's mind from actual physical condition of the premises.

The argument in favour of an assumption of both landlord and tenant having complied with their respective covenants is perhaps more controversial. On the one hand it may enable a disreputable landlord to benefit from a breach of, for instance, his obligations to repair the roof and structure by nevertheless reviewing the open market rental value for the premises on the assumption that the disrepairs do not exist. (The tenant would of course have some remedy by suing the landlord under the terms of the lease for breach of covenant.) On the other hand, it is argued: taking account of the landlord's failure to repair and assessing a lower rent may act as a major disincentive for the landlord to carry out the repairs after the rent review has taken place and may in fact lead to the landlord carrying out unnecessary "repairs"/improvements (and probably recharging the cost to the tenant if there is a service charge in the lease) prior to any rent review simply to make sure of avoiding this risk.

Occupation and goodwill of tenant
As mentioned earlier these matters are usually and quite fairly disregarded. Without such disregards there is a real risk that the tenant may end up paying a high rent for reasons unconnected with any underlying increase in property values. If there is no disregard of the tenant's occupation and the goodwill of his business, in the real world, there is every likelihood that, at least a successful tenant, will be willing to pay over and above the open market rental value of his premises merely to maintain continuity of occupation for his business.

Improvements
In the absence of any express assumption, improvements (whether carried out by the landlord or the tenant) will be valued and, assuming they enhance the value of the premises, are likely to result in a higher rental value being assessed for those premises.

In practice, most improvements are carried out by tenants. They will not be happy if, having paid the initial cost of the relevant improvement, they are then penalised by paying a higher rent following a rent review because they have enhanced the value of the premises. The best solution from the tenant's point of view is to include a disregard of improvements. However, this may have the unforeseen effect of assuming, for instance, premises that do not comply with fire regulations (assuming the improvement to be a fire escape). In such circumstances the best compromise solution is probably to ignore only those improvements which have the effect of increasing the open market rental value for the premises. This avoids any question as to whether one has (by disregarding all improvements) to value premises which cannot legally be used without the improvement yet represents a fair protection to any tenant.

Often rent review clauses seek to ignore improvements carried out pursuant to an obligation to the landlord. The intention in many cases is to exclude "improvements" carried out pursuant to an agreement for lease where, for instance, a retail tenant has taken over a "shell" finished unit and shop fitted it to suit its own requirements. Provided that the lease doesn't (expressly or impliedly) exclude reference to improvements carried out before the date of the lease, the shop-fitting works will be carried out pursuant to an obligation to the landlord and, to the extent that they constitute an improvement will be excluded from the valuation of the open market rental value of the premises. In such circumstances, this is probably perfectly reasonable since the tenant is quite likely to have been compensated for the carrying out of its works by a rent-free period. The unforeseen danger is that most leases will include an obligation on tenants to carry out any works that may be required pursuant to statute. For instance, under fire regulations a tenant may be required to install a separate fire escape to allow alternative emergency access from upper floors. Such an improvement, if carried out pursuant to a requirement in the lease to comply with statutes will also be carried out pursuant to an obligation to the landlord, namely the obligation in the lease to comply with statutes. Such an improvement would therefore not be disregarded.

Disregard of rent-free periods
In the absence of any express assumption, since the decision in *99 Bishopsgate Ltd* v *Prudential Assurance Co Ltd* [1985] 1 EGLR 72, it has been accepted that if, in the open market, tenants would expect to receive a rent-free period as part of the consideration for paying a particular open market rent, the value of this rent-free period should be taken into account when assessing the open market rent for the particular premises.

To counteract this argument, there is often an express disregard of any rent-free periods that may be granted in the open market to compensate a tenant for the time taken to carry out its fitting-out works. The obvious justification is that the existing tenant has already shop fitted the premises and probably obtained a rent-free period while he was so doing, and should not, therefore, receive the further benefit of a reduced rent at review to reflect the fact that other tenants in the open market would need to re shop-fit the premises to suit their particular needs.

The wording of such disregards has to be looked at carefully. While it may well be fair to disregard rent-free periods being given in the open market to compensate tenants for their costs of shop fitting (assuming the particular tenant has already been allowed such a concession), a blanket disregard of all rent-free periods and other rent concessions may work injustice. This may be the case where in the open market the rental concessions are being offered not to compensate the tenant for the time it will take to shop fit, but rather to induce the tenant to enter into the lease at all. For instance a reverse premium or rent-free period may be offered in the open market in order to attract tenants to pay a rent that would otherwise be higher than the open market rental value for the particular premises.

By way of an example, if we assume a 25-year lease on offer with five-yearly reviews. If the open market rent for the premises is £10,000 pa, but the landlord is prepared to grant a rent free period for the first six months of the term and after that would require a rent of £10,200 pa, any tenant in the open market would be receiving a real discount for the first five years if he accepted the higher rent and the rent-free period for six months (the difference being five years at £10,000 pa = £50,000 total as against 54 months at £10,200 pa = £45,900). It might well suit the landlord to enter into such an arrangement if this particular review was likely to be used as evidence of open market rental value for similar premises: so long as evidence of the rent-free period was not publicised, the landlord might claim that the open market rental value for similar premises should be based on a level equating to £10,200 pa and not £10,000 pa!

It is therefore important for a tenant to realise the differences between rent concessions being offered in the open market purely to cover the cost of shop fitting and rent concessions being offered in the open market which are intended as inducement for potential tenants to pay a higher rent. While the former may fairly be disregarded, it will not usually be fair to disregard the latter.

Once the latter type of inducement has been identified there is no single accepted methodology for adjusting the headline rent to find out the underlying rent. One argument is that you get a rent inducement as a one off payment for taking a 20 or 25-year lease and therefore it is written off over 20 or 25 years.

The opposing view is that the concession is enjoyed in the period up to the first review and at first review a full open market rent will be fixed. The benefit is therefore amortised over the period up to review. It may be fair to say that this is a tenant's interpretation while the former is a landlord's stance.

There is an argument that rent-free period (and certainly capital payments) pass out of both the landlord's and the tenant's accounts once their financial year end is passed. Working examples of this situation are shown in *City Offices plc* v *Bryanston Insurance Co Ltd*; *City Offices plc* v *Allianz Cornhill International Insurance Co* [1993] 11 EG 129.

9.2 Time periods under rent review clauses

Following the major decision of the House of Lords in the case of *United Scientific Holdings Ltd* v *Burnley Borough Council* (1977) 243 EG 43 the overriding assumption in all rent review clauses is that time is not "of the essence" (ie failure to keep to a particular time limit is not vital) unless: (i) time is expressly stated to be of the essence; or (ii) the inter-relation of the rent review clause and other clauses in the lease make time of the essence; or (iii) the tenant suffers undue hardship due to the lateness of the review.

In many older rent review clauses it is not uncommon to see a time-scale for the taking of different steps (usually the service by the landlord of a notice requiring a rent review and suggesting a level of reviewed rent, followed by the service by the tenant of a counternotice either agreeing the landlord's suggested rent or else referring the determination of the rent to an independent valuer). Often, in old forms of rent review clause the time periods for taking the appropriate steps are expressly stated to be of the essence. For instance, the tenant may have one month from the date of service of the landlord's notice in which to serve his counternotice. Failure to serve this counternotice within the one-month period (even if only a day late) may have the effect that the rent suggested in the landlord's notice is deemed to have been accepted as the reviewed rent. Note however that use of words such as "shall" ("the tenant shall have one month in which to serve a counter-notice stating . . .") is not of itself sufficient to make time of the essence. These are commonly known as deeming provisions.

The only common situation where time is not expressly stated to be of the essence, but may nevertheless be deemed to be of the essence is the situation where there is a clause allowing the tenant to predetermine the lease, ie a break clause. Where the tenant has the right to terminate the lease on a particular date (which is intended to be after the date on which a rent review has either been determined or at least after the date on which a landlord's notice of the suggested rent should have been served) time may become "of the essence" in relation to the determination of the rent or the service of the landlord's notice. The reasoning is that the tenant is intended to exercise its right to predetermine the lease knowing of the reviewed rent or at least the landlord's opinion of the reviewed rent, and has only one chance to exercise the break.

There are a number of cases on the inter-relationship of a break clause and rent review clause which are not entirely consistent. For instance, in the case of *Al Saloom* v *Shirley James Travel Service Ltd* (1981) 259 EG 420 the exercise of both the break clause and rent review clause required not less than six month's prior written notice on the respective parts of the tenant and the landlord. The landlord failed to serve his rent review notice on time and the Court of Appeal held that he had thereby lost his right to review, time being of the essence. By contrast, in the more recent case of *Metrolands Investments Ltd* v *J H Dewhurst Ltd* [1986] 1 EGLR 125 the rent review clause provided for a reviewed rent to be agreed by the parties or else determined by an independent arbitrator on or before August 18 1981. The break clause provided that the tenant could exercise its right to break by notice given between August 19 and November 18 1981 (ie after the rent review should have been determined). The Court of Appeal took the view that the obtaining of the arbitrator's determination of the reviewed rent could not, as a matter of practice, be guaranteed to be received on or before August 18 1981. Furthermore, the potential hardship suffered by the tenant as a result of the landlord's late instigation of the rent review provisions (on December 2 1981) could have been overcome by the tenant instigating the rent review provisions itself (as it was entitled to do under the terms of the lease). In the circumstances, the time for the exercise of the rent review was held not to be of the essence.

The rationale to be drawn from these cases is perhaps that the courts will look to the relative hardship to the parties if time is held to be of the essence and to the opportunities either party had to circumvent that hardship. A further example is shown in *Holicater Ltd* v *Grandred Ltd* [1993] 23 EG 129.

9.3   Restrictions on use

As previously mentioned, in the absence of express words to the contrary, the permitted use under the lease will be assumed to be the only use when considering the open market rental value of the particular premises at rent review.

The courts have recognised that a particularly restrictive user clause (eg not to use premises other than for the business of the particular tenant) may have a depressing effect on rent since, in the

open market, there are fewer potential tenants ab'
premises for the permitted use and fewer still who '
take a long lease with a restrictive user in view of the difficulties
might face in trying to assign their lease at a later date: see for
example *Plinth Property Investments Ltd* v *Mott, Hay & Anderson*
(1978) 249 EG 1167.

However, where a particularly restrictive use is qualified so as to
allow the tenant to change the permitted use of the premises "with
the consent of the landlord, such consent not to be unreasonably
withheld", the courts have held that a valuer is fully entitled to take
into account a use not presently being carried on by the tenant, but
which might be carried on (on the basis that the landlord could not
unreasonably withhold consent to it) when assessing the open
market rental value of the premises. For example, if a lease permits
use of a premises as a butchers shop or, with the prior written
consent of the landlord, such consent not to be unreasonably
withheld, for any other type of shop, a valuer will not be restricted
to looking solely at the level of rent that other butchers might be
prepared to pay for the particular premises, but can legitimately
look at the sort of rents that shop keepers in general might be
prepared to pay for the particular premises. An example of this
approach can be seen in the case of *Aldwych Club Ltd* v *Copthall
Property Co Ltd* (1962) 185 EG 219.

Conceptual difficulties have arisen where a particularly restrictive
user clause restricts the user of the premises by reference to the
tenant's business. This restriction may be worded, for example, not
to use the premises "otherwise than as offices in connection with
the tenant's business" or may define the particular tenant's
business: see for instance *London Scottish Properties* v *Council for
Professionals Associated with Medicine* unreported November 8
1979, where the tenants were not permitted to use the premises
"otherwise than as offices in connection with the [tenant's] business
*for the purposes of the Council for Professions Supplementary to
Medicine*".

With either clause, it could be argued that the leases were
unassignable and that therefore any valuer should assess simply
the rent that the particular tenant in occupation would be prepared
to pay knowing that it could not assign its lease.

To get round the problem of assessing (entirely subjectively) what
the particular tenant might be prepared to pay by way of rent, the
courts have construed restrictions on use of premises in connection

with a particular tenant's business to have the effect that rent is to be assessed on the basis that any potential tenant in the open market would have permission for use of the premises for its particular business, but would not subsequently be able to apply for a change of this use to enable it to assign to a tenant carrying on a different business. There is thus still a strongly depressing effect on the open market rental value.

9.4 Restrictions on alienation

Closely allied to restrictions on user are restrictions in the particular lease against alienation, ie assigning or underletting of the particular premises.

Where there is an absolute prohibition against assigning or underletting and the lease is thus personal to the particular tenant, in order to assess the open market rental value for the premises it has to be assumed that any potential tenant's wish to occupy the premises will be tempered by the realisation that he will not be able to subsequently assign or underlet the premises. If the lease is for more than a short term, the open market rental value of the premises is likely to be depressed.

Similarly, where a consent to assign or underlet is conditional upon obtaining landlord's consent "consent not to be unreasonably withheld", the likelihood of obtaining landlord's consent in the majority of cases will have the effect that the open market rental value of the premises should not be depressed.

Where a sublease permits alienation, subject to landlord's consent, it does not imply that the headlandlords consent will be forthcoming. He can be as unreasonable as he wishes. These circumstances give rise to a reduction in open market rent to reflect this fetter on alienation.

9.5 Expert or arbitrator

Most rent review clauses will contain some provision for a determination of a reviewed rent by an independent valuer in the event that the parties cannot reach agreement by a certain date. Such independent valuer will either act as an expert or as an arbitrator, depending on the terms of the particular rent review clause. Sometimes, the landlord will be given a choice as to whether the independent valuer should act as an expert or an arbitrator.

The main difference between an independent valuer acting as an expert or as an arbitrator is that in the former case, he is relying on his own expertise as an "expert" in rent review matters to determine the reviewed rent. The lease may contain provisions allowing the parties to make representations to him as to what they believe the reviewed rent should be but, ultimately, it is entirely a matter for the valuer to use his own expert knowledge to decide his view of what the reviewed rent should be.

In the case of arbitration, the valuer must conduct an arbitration in accordance with the Arbitration Acts which provide a formal framework for both parties to make representations to the arbitrator, and for the arbitrator to decide, on the basis of those representations, what the reviewed rent should be. The arbitrator must not be seen to rely upon his own expert knowledge and is (theoretically at least) confined to the rental evidence produced to him by the parties.

There are various perceived advantages and disadvantages of both forms of valuation which can be grouped under the following headings:

Cost
It is often argued that an independent valuer acting as an expert costs less than an independent valuer acting as an arbitrator. In both cases, the parties will be responsible for the valuer's fees but, in the case of expert determination, there is no form of procedure to be complied with and, since the expert is essentially using his own knowledge, it may be possible to obtain a quicker decision. However, if both parties appoint their own surveyors to make representations to the independent expert valuer, the costs to the parties can very quickly mount. There is a growing tendency among experts to elaborate and embellish the expert procedure so that it is very little different to an oral arbitration in terms of time and cost.

Furthermore, a rent review arbitration conducted on the basis of written submissions from both sides (thus avoiding the costs of a full arbitration hearing) may well not exceed the costs of a single independent expert.

Because an independent expert may have to assemble his own information and (unlike an arbitrator) may be potentially liable in negligence, he may be justified in charging a higher fee than if he were acting as an arbitrator. Furthermore, the fees of an arbitrator can be taxed by the court unless they have been previously fixed by an agreement in writing.

Speed
As mentioned above, there is a perception that an independent valuer acting as an expert will be able to reach a decision more quickly than an independent valuer acting as an arbitrator. However, if both parties are permitted to, and do, make representations to the expert, there may be very little difference between an expert determination or an arbitration.

Clear rules of procedure
Because an arbitration will be subject to the rules set out in the Arbitration Acts, both parties will be given an adequate opportunity to make their case before the arbitrator. This may not necessarily be the case with an expert determination.

Most arbitrations are dealt with (with the agreement of the parties) by written representations. In more contentious cases or where there is a larger rent at stake, there is much to recommend an oral hearing. In particular, provided you are confident in your case, it can be very helpful indeed to cross-examine the other sides expert witness when he is under oath.

Hearings
An independent valuer acting as an arbitrator has powers to compel the disclosure of all relevant documents in the possession of the parties and the attendance of witnesses at an oral hearing where they can be cross-examined.

In complicated cases where either large sums of money are involved or where the particular rent review clause is less than clear, the Arbitration Acts make provision for the determination of preliminary points of law by the courts. Conversely, where an independent valuer is acting as an expert, a separate application for a declaration on a point of law has to be made to the High Court, which is both costly and time consuming.

Power to require reasons
An arbitrator will normally give reasons for his award if requested by the parties. Conversely, an expert is under no duty to give reasons for his determination unless the provisions of the particular rent review clause require him to do so. A perceived advantage with arbitration is therefore that the parties can understand why a particular reviewed rent has been arrived at rather than feeling that the final figure has been "plucked from the air"! There is however an

amount of trepidation about requesting a reasoned award, for fear it will be an unbreakable precedent in terms of valuation approach for subsequent reviews.

Note however that the 1979 Arbitration Act and subsequent case law has sought to limit the circumstances in which the parties to a rent review arbitration can appeal against an arbitrator's determination.

CHAPTER 10

Issue of dilapidations

10.1 Legal framework

The starting point must be the lease. However you cannot sensibly interpret repairing obligations without knowing how they will be approached by the courts.

Although there are a wide variety of words used in defining a repairing obligation such as "rebuild", "replace", "renew", etc. the tendency has been for the court to adopt exactly the same approach to the standard of repair, whatever formula of words is employed.

In order to extend it, a more detailed provision would normally be required.

It has proved difficult over recent years to identify any meaningful guidance from the court's approach as to what is within and what is beyond the scope of "repair".

Three main points have appeared:

- Premises have to have deteriorated from a previous better condition for the question of disrepair to arise at all.
- It is the remedial scheme, not the nature or cause of the defects or damage which the courts will address.
- The remedial scheme has to be appraised according to the ordinary everyday meaning of the word "repair".

Deterioration from previous condition

In the case of *Post Office* v *Aquarius Properties Ltd* [1987] 1 EGLR 40 evidence was produced that when the building was first constructed, poor workmanship and possibly poor design, had resulted in porous concrete and defective construction joints which allowed water to get into the basement of the premises. Between 1979 and 1984 following a rise in the water table the basement had been permanently ankle-deep in water. The water table then fell and the basement dried out. It was held that there was no evidence of disrepair at the date of trial and therefore no obligation to take steps to prevent the basement from flooding if the water table rose again.

This seems to contradict the long-standing tenet that a covenant "to keep" premises in repair includes putting them into repair, if they are not in repair at the start of the tenancy: see *Proudfoot* v *Hart* (1890) 25 QBD 42.

The reconcilation is that the rule does not apply if there has been no deterioration in the premises during the period from their construction. In the *Post Office* case the defects had been present throughout the life of the building – there had been no earlier better condition.

The moral here is that the landlord who wants his tenant to put the premises into repair must either include a very clear and express covenant to this effect or show that at some time before the tenant took the premises they were in a better state than they were when let.

This raises the question as to how far repair will include renewal. In *Ravenseft Properties Ltd* v *Davstone (Holdings) Ltd* (1978) 249 EG 51, there was a partial collapse of the exterior stone cladding of a leasehold block of flats owing to their inherent faulty construction. The tenant's defence was that where a want of repair was caused by some inherent defect it could never fall within the covenant to repair. It was held that the true test of liability was that it was a question of fact and degree whether what the tenant was being asked to do was to repair or whether it involved giving back to the landlord a wholly different thing from that demised.

In applying this test the proportion which the cost of the disputed work bears to the value or the cost of the whole premises was a helpful guide. The cost of rectifying the inherent defect in the *Ravenseft* case was held to form a trivial part of the cost of the whole building and did not amount to such a change in its character as to take the costs outside the ambit of the tenants covenant to repair.

In the case of *Plough Investments Ltd* v *Manchester City Council* [1989] 1 EGLR 244, rusting to the steel super structure of a 1920s property, if allowed to continue would probably result in cracking, spalling and displacement of the brickwork. The building was occupied by a number of commercial tenants who contributed towards the landlord's obligation to keep the exterior of the building in repair through a service charge.

The court held that there would be no disrepair to the steel frame until such time (if any) as the rust reduced the strength of the steel and there would be no disrepair to the exterior until such time as the rusting of the steel frame threatened to damage it by cracking and moving it. Even if it were shown that the whole frame was damaged, the treatment scheme on the scale advised to the landlord was likely to be beyond the scope of repair.

There was evidence of rusting to the steel frame which manifested itself in cracking and displacement of bricks. The landlords decided to commission a full structural survey which encompassed a separate report by a firm of structural engineers. As a result, a scheme was devised to expose all steel work in external walls and shot-blast it to remove any rust and then to treat the steel and recover it in concrete. The scheme would have cost between £383,553 and £507,999. The landlord sought to recover these costs as costs of repair under the service charge. The tenant's commissioned their own experts report which suggested the landlords' proposed works were excessive.

The court found as follows:

- That the landlords' proposed works were excessive and went beyond repair.
- That the cost of the landlords' report on the proposed works was also not recoverable because it was not incurred for the particular purpose of remedying some particular condition of apparent disrepair, but instead it was a report commissioned by way of a general survey to see if any disrepair was present.

This case would seem to make it clear that repair does not cover preventative work and that a landlord wishing to recover pursuant to his repairing obligation would be well advised to produce a scheme of temporary work dealing with areas which are patently damaged.

Notices

Before trying to forfeit for non-repair, a landlord has to serve a notice under section 146 of the Law of Property Act 1925. That notice has to:

- Specify the particular breach complained of.
- State that the tenant is required to remedy the breach.
- Require the tenant to make compensation in money terms.

The section does not require the landlord to state a time-period within which the work has to be done.

The best approach is to require the tenant to remedy the breach "within a reasonable time". If you specify an actual period, you open up a number of potential problems.

If you put any period into the notice and proceedings are brought at the end of that period and are dismissed because a reasonable time has not yet elapsed, you may not simply wait the extra time the court thinks reasonable and then issue a new writ, but rather may have to serve a fresh section 146 notice and allow time for the work to be done before issuing that writ, just as if you had allowed no time.

Second, a well-advised tenant challenging such a notice will argue that he has to investigate the schedule which the landlord has produced and get his own advice on it, prepare a specification and, in the case of all but very small works put the matter out to tender, consider the tenders received, enter into a contract, etc. You therefore have to make provision for these preliminaries as well as the duration of works.

You may encounter a series of breaches which will take different periods of time to remedy. The answer is to serve a number of notices and then seek to forfeit on the basis of the one that needs the shortest time for compliance.

Tenants who have three or more years of their leases unexpired are of course in a favoured position under the provisions of the Leasehold Property (Repairs) Act 1938. No action for forfeiture or damages can be brought against them unless a section 146 notice containing the information required by the 1938 Act has been served and either no counternotice has been given by the tenant or the leave of the court is obtained by the landlord on one of the grounds set out in section 1(5).

10.2 The schedule and the cost of work

A schedule of dilapidation or wants of repair is normally prepared by a chartered building surveyor. There are essentially two types of schedule being an interim schedule and a terminal schedule.

An interim schedule is prepared during the term of the lease, usually with the specific intention of having the tenant comply with his repairing obligation. They are notoriously difficult to enforce.

The terminal schedule is prepared at the expiry of the lease with the view to either having the tenant reinstate the building to the condition he should have left it in or alternatively to make a claim for liquidated damages.

A schedule of dilapidations, either interim or terminal, is a catalogue of defects which are to be made good in order for the tenant to comply with the repairing covenants. It does not describe in detail the method of carrying out the repair or redecoration and is not therefore a specification for obtaining a builder's estimate.

A schedule will be served on the tenant in accordance with the procedure under the Law of Property Act 1925, section 164(1) in the case of an interim or terminal schedule. If it is a terminal schedule it should be served on the tenant with a claim for damages for breach of contract.

The vast majority of dilapidations claims are settled by negotiation between the respective building surveyors of the landlord and the tenant. There are two statutory ceilings to tenant's liability for damages for disrepair, both to be found in section 18 of the Landlord and Tenant Act 1927.

10.3 Diminution in the value of the reversion

Section 18 (1) of the Landlord and Tenant Act 1927 imposes a statutory ceiling on liquidated damages for dilapidations:

Damages for a breach of a covenant or agreement to keep or put premises in repair at the termination of a lease, or to leave or put premises in repair at the termination of a lease, whether such covenant or agreement is expressed or implied, and whether general or specific, shall in no case exceed the amount (if any) by which the value of the reversion (whether immediate or not) in the premises is diminished owing to the breach of such covenant or agreement as aforesaid.

For these purposes the everyday meaning of the key words apply as follows:

Diminution   =   Decrease or dwindling.
Reversion   =   That part of a grantors estate or interest in property
                 left after the grant of some lesser interest, eg the
                 interest of a freeholder after granting a lease.

So the valuer's task is to assess the impact of the tenant's disrepair on the value of the landlord's interest, which for the purpose of this discussion is treated as a freehold. The longer the unexpired balance on the tenant's lease, the less the effect on the freehold interest. This is why most diminution valuations occur at lease expiry in assessing liquidated damages on terminal schedules of dilapidations.

A simple approach to finding the loss actually suffered by the landlord is to assess the cost of disrepair plus a sum for loss of rent while the work is done. However, cost does not equal value. Proof of this is that the cost of building an office block would be similar in Bristol, London or Glasgow; but the value would be vastly different. In some cases, however, cost is the best measure of diminution, although usually it is not.

In order to recover damages, the landlord must prove diminution in the value of the reversion due to non-repair at least equal to the amount of damages claimed. Evidence of the cost of repairs is not necessarily evidence of diminution.

The usual method of assessment of damages is to take the value of the reversion as it is with the breach of repairing covenants and take it as it would be if there were no breach ie a before and after valuation. The difference between the two values is the limit of the damages which can be recovered and represents the diminution in the value of the reversion.

Of course, if the actual cost of the works is less, then the damages will be the lower amount.

Example 1

10,000 sq ft, 1930s factory on a 5-acre site in an area with very poor industrial demand. Cost of works – £500,000

Value in good repair

Area	100,000 sq ft	
Rent psf	£1.25	
ERV	£125,000 pa	
YP perp @ 15%	6.66	
		£833,333
		Say £835,000

Value in disrepair

Area	100,000 sq ft	
Rent psf	£1.00	
ERV	£100,000 pa	
YP perp @ 17%	5.88	
		£588,000
		Say £590,000
		Diminution £245,000

In these circumstances damages are considerably less than cost but, nevertheless, are substantial.

Example 2

Office building where the demised space is inefficiently laid out, being subdivided into small cellular offices. Cost of repairs to existing layout – £200,000.

Value with tenants repairing liability fulfilled

Existing net lettable area	20,000 sq ft	
Rent psf	£10.00	
ERV	£200,000 pa	
YP perp @ 10%	10	
		£2,000,000

Value in existing condition

Net lettable area after refurbishment	25,000 sq ft	
Rent psf	£10.00	
ERV	£250,000	
YP perp @ 9%	11.1111	
Gross development value		£2,777,777

Less cost of refurbishment:

1. Building costs	
2. Supervision fees	
3. Interim finance	£600,000
4. Letting fees/promotion	
5. Funding fees	
6. Developers profit	
Residual value	£2,177,777
	Say £2,175,000
	Diminution +£175,000

In this example, the refurbishment potential outweighs the value of the current layout in good repair and reduces damages to nil.

The circumstances in example 2 are specifically covered by section 18:

> and in particular no damage shall be recovered for a breach of any such covenant or agreement to leave or put premises in repair at the termination of a lease, if it is shown that the premises, in whatever state of repair they might be, would at or shortly after the termination of the tenancy, have been or be pulled down, or such structural alterations made therein as would render valueless the repairs covered by the covenant or agreement.

However, this only applies if the value of tenant's works is totally obviated by the redevelopment. In a demolition situation damages will always be nil. There, if acting for a landlord, it can pay to defer redevelopment proposals until the dilapidations claim is settled since the tenant must prove that the landlord had made a definite decision or had a definite intention to pull the building down.

So, if we revisit example 1, but add the further diminution that a DIY retailer will pay £400,000 an acre for a cleared 5-acre site, then, assuming planning, this site is worth around £2,000,000 and damages would be nil. If acting for a tenant, always be vigilant when dealing with large old buildings that may have redevelopment potential.

You may also encounter a refurbishment situation where the value of the dilapidations works is not cancelled by the refurbishment.

Example 2B

If in example 2 the cost of repairs had been £200,000 for internal works and £150,000 for roof repairs and stone cleaning, then the following valuations would apply:

Value in existing condition

Gross development value (as before)	£2,775,000	
Less cost of refurbishment	£600,000	
Open market value		£2,175,000

Value with tenant's repairs completed

Gross development value (as before)	£2,775,000	
Less cost of refurbishment		
(£600,000 as before but less the cost		
of the roof and stone work – £150,000)	£450,000	
Open market value		£2,325,000
Diminution		£150,000

In this example damages equal the cost of those tenants works which are not "rendered valueless" by the structural alterations.

Example 3

Shop premises in small market town in very poor order. Market is weak and most sales are to owner occupiers. Costs of works – £35,000

Value in repair

			£
Ground floor	500 sq ft (ITZA)	@ £15.00 =	7,500
First floor	700 sq ft	@ £ 1.50 =	1,050
Basement	400 sq ft	@ £ 1.00 =	400
			8,950
ERV			9,000 pa
YP perp @ 12%			8.333
			75,000

Value in disrepair

Owner occupier will pay open market value with works complete, less the cost to him of doing the works, ie:

$$£75,000 – £35,000 = £40,000$$

Thus the diminution in the value of the reversion is the cost of works.

Generally, where the premises can be relet for the same purposes as before and at the same rent, provided that the repairs which the tenant ought to have done are carried out, or where the repairs ought to be done as a matter of prudent estate management, or where the landlord takes possession of the premises himself, the measure of damages is the cost of works.

TACTICS FOR LEASE RENEWAL

CHAPTER 11

Right to renew

The Landlord and Tenant Act 1954, Part II contains various provisions for security of tenure so that in certain circumstances a business tenant will have the right to renew his lease. However, the tactics adopted by the landlord and his use of the procedure under the Act in the period running up to the end of the lease and while new terms are being negotiated will affect the nature and quality of the deal the landlord achieves if and when the lease is finally renewed.

A general summary of the relevant provisions is as follows:

- Where a tenant occupies business premises it has security of tenure such that the tenancy continues after the contractual term expires subject to certain exceptions.
- The landlord can only end the tenancy by following the procedures in the 1954 Act.
- In any event the tenant can apply to the court for a new lease which the landlord can only oppose on certain grounds in section 30 of the Act.
- The tenant can start the renewal process by requesting a new lease from the landlord under section 26 of the Act.
- If terms cannot be agreed for the new lease then the Act regulates what those terms are.
- Where the landlord is able to successfully oppose the grant of a new lease on grounds where the tenant is not at fault that tenant may receive compensation for disturbance.

However, one of the key issues for the landlord will be how to make tactical use of the procedure under the Act and its provisions to achieve the best deal possible.

11.1 Tactics to avoid the 1954 Act

The first issue for the landlord to consider is whether there are circumstances in which the Act can be either excluded or avoided. The key point to note at this stage is the considerable difference between the landlord's negotiating position on the grant of a new lease and on a lease renewal. On the grant of a new lease the landlord is able to dictate terms subject only to market forces. On a lease renewal a landlord negotiates in the context of the tenant's security of tenure where this applies under the Act. If, on a lease renewal, the landlord wishes to take away the tenants' security of tenure this will only be achievable as part of a negotiated settlement; a trade-off between the respective interests of landlord and tenant.

The Act applies to any tenancy where the premises are occupied by the tenant for the purpose of its business or for that and other purposes (section 23). Within the strict limits of section 23 of the Act the landlord should consider, both on the grant of a new lease or on the renewal of an existing lease under the Act the commercial and tactical benefit if any to be derived from the following:

• Whether a licence or tenancy at will may be granted.
• Whether the nature of the occupation by the tenant qualifies or on a lease renewal still qualifies under the Act.
• Whether the nature of the tenant's business still falls within that protected by the Act.
• Whether on the grant of the lease any of the statutory exclusions apply.
• Whether on a lease renewal or on the grant of a lease the exclusion of the Act by court order can be built in as part of the negotiations.

A licence or tenancy at will

The tenant has no security of tenure under the Act if the occupation is by way of a genuine licence or tenancy at will.

However, the decision to use either to avoid the Act must be accompanied by a warning: there is a risk that if such arrangements are found to be a sham, then the tenant will enjoy full security under the Act where the qualifying conditions are otherwise fulfilled. Where the arrangements are genuine, however, the Act will not apply – *Addiscombe Garden Estates Ltd v Crabbe* [1958] 1 QB 513 and *Wheeler v Mercer* [1957] AC 416.

A licence is a personal right to occupy premises on a non-exclusive basis as opposed to a tenancy which creates a legal interest in the premises and grants the right to exclusive possession. It is the element of exclusive possession which primarily determines whether the nature of the occupation is a tenancy or a licence and this principle applies despite what the parties may allege is the basis for the occupation or how it is documented: see *Antoniades* v *Villiers* [1988] 2 EGLR 78 and *AG Securities* v *Vaughan* [1988] 2 EGLR 78.

The legal difference between a tenancy and licence is arguable in the context of business licences (see *Dresden Estates Ltd* v *Collinson* [1987] 1 EGLR 45) and so the landlord who can avoid the Act as part of the negotiations should not use a licence at all. The better option is to exclude the Act by court order.

A tenancy at will is an arrangement whereby the tenant has exclusive possession of the premises, but does not have the certainty of a fixed term or agreed period: instead the tenant remains at the premises for so long as the landlord permits.

In the context of the tenancy at will there are also good reasons why it is not a commercial alternative: the absence of a certain term or period of occupation will not appeal to the business tenant since the tenant's occupation will be at the will of the landlord; and a court may be unable to distinguish between the tenancy at will and a tenancy under the Act, especially if the rent is collected on a periodic basis. The consequence may be a tenancy protected by the Act.

The tactical and practical use of the tenancy at will is to assist negotiations and to allow a tenant into occupation pending the grant of an exclusion order, or as part of the pre-completion negotiations: see *Javad* v *Aqil* [1990] 2 EGLR 82.

There may be circumstances where terms had been agreed for a lease excluded from the Act, but the documentation is not quite ready or, indeed, where the tenant urgently needs occupation and, while the principles have been settled between landlord and tenant, the details of the lease are still being negotiated: these are circumstances where the tenant may take occupation of the premises as tenant at will pending the completion of the lease and the grant of the exclusion order. It would however be vital to document that occupation to make it clear that the tenant remains at the premises at the will of the landlord until the lease is completed: see *Cardiothoracic Institute* v *Shrewdcrest Ltd* [1986] 2 EGLR 57.

How the tenant occupies the premises
The landlord also needs to be aware of the way in which the tenant is occupying the premises during the lease, since on renewal this

may affect the extent to which the tenant still qualifies under the Act and consequently the tactical advantage that this may bring in negotiating the renewal lease.

The tenant must occupy the premises during the renewal proceedings – *Wandsworth London Borough* v *Singh* [1991] 2 EGLR 75, but the nature of the occupation has been defined at law so that a tenant may make tactical use of the permitted occupation to retain security of tenure while not in full occupation.

It is important for the landlord to appreciate the extent to which the tenant can be absent from the premises and still retain security of tenure. The tenant does not have to be present in person at the premises but can run the business operations through an agent or manager – *Cafeteria (Keighley) Ltd* v *Harrison* (1956) 168 EG 668.

The landlord also needs to be aware, when it comes to renew the lease, of whether the tenant has changed the structure of the business: a move from sole trader or partnership to a limited company status or amalgamation or reconstruction of companies may mean that the business is being run by a body or person different from that named in the lease. Without a proper assignment or sublease, there may be some tactical advantage in the renewal negotiations for the landlord to claim either that the tenant is in breach of the lease (where it prohibits assigning or subletting without landlords prior consent) or that the tenant has lost its security of tenure under the Act as being a body or person other than the tenant is in occupation – *Nozari-Zadeh* v *Pearl Assurance plc* [1987] 2 EGLR 91.

The tenant's business

The next issue for the landlord to consider on lease renewal is whether the tenant's business qualifies or still qualifies for protection under the Act and the extent to which that can be built into the renewal negotiations. The Act requires that the tenant occupies the premises for the purpose of a business carried on by it or for that and other purposes (section 23). The definition of business includes not only a trade profession or employment but also activities carried on by incorporated and unincorporated bodies. This means that the profit motive does not have to be present for the activity to qualify as a business: a non-profit making activity will also qualify – *Hills (Patents) Ltd* v *University College Hospital Board of Governors* [1956] 1 QB 90 and also *Methodist Secondary Schools Trust Deed Trustees* v *O'Leary* [1993] 16 EG 119.

The landlord also needs to keep a check on the extent to which there are any non-business uses at the premises. While a mixture of residential and business use will not be fatal to the tenant losing security of tenure under the Act, the tenant will only be protected while the business use remains a primary use and if it becomes ancillary to the other use (whether residential or not), security of tenure may be lost, thus putting the landlord in a stronger position on lease renewal: see *Gurton* v *Parrott* [1991] 1 EGLR 98.

11.2 Tactical use of statutory exceptions

A landlord can make tactical use of the statutory exceptions to ensure the tenant has no security of tenure where market forces or negotiations permit; or where the tenant's circumstances have changed to make such exceptions available as a commercial alternative.

The exceptions are set out in section 43 and, on a lease renewal, the following are relevant as tactics to avoid the business tenant's statutory right to renew:

- A written service tenancy.
- A fixed-term tenancy for less than six months, but not if the tenancy provides for renewal beyond that six months and not if the tenant has occupied the premises for more than 12 months (including any period during which his predecessor was there).

11.3 Excluding the 1954 Act by court order

This is less of a tactic and more of a mechanism under the Act to exclude a tenant's security of tenure. However, it has tactical use in negotiations often as a trade-off on the grant of the lease or on renewal.

In a depressed market a tenant may trade security of tenure for some other benefit under the lease, such as a tenant's break clause, assured that the landlord would not want to lose his tenant on renewal if the market is still depressed. However, the landlord will have secured a tactical and commercial advantage if the market improves during the term. That, of course, is a gamble.

The landlord and tenant make a joint court application to exclude sections 24 to 28 inclusive of the Act. The application to the court can be made by both parties jointly either to the High Court or the county court since both have jurisdiction to make such an order. From July 1 1991 the county court is able to deal with all premises regardless of the rateable value and in most cases will be the more convenient method of obtaining the order.

It is usual for the application to be made by the solicitors acting for the landlord and tenant although the court will deal with an application where the parties are acting in person. In circumstances where the tenant is acting in person the court will want to be sure that the tenant has not been forced into this arrangement. Where the tenant is acting in person the court may be more likely to require the parties to attend. In such circumstances and to try to avoid attendance (thus saving time and expense) the court application may be accompanied by a letter from the tenant to the court confirming its consent to the order being made in the terms sought and confirming that it understands its effect. In most cases the court will make the order without either party having to attend but neither party should assume that this is merely a rubber-stamping exercise. The application has to be submitted in a form which convinces the court that the tenant's rights have been taken into account in the negotiations between the parties and that the tenant having regard to the circumstances considers that it will be reasonable for it to lose its right to renew. If there are special circumstances which explain why the tenant should not have the right to renew under the Act in the proposed lease then these should also be set out in the court application to assist the court in making its decision.

Here are some examples:

- Where the landlord intends to redevelop or refurbish the premises when the lease ends.
- Where the tenant only needs the premises for a temporary or short term purpose.
- Where there is a superior landlord who has only authorised subletting on the basis that the sublease is excluded from the Act.
- Where the premises are temporarily surplus to the landlord's immediate needs, but may be required subsequently for its own use.

The order has to be for a fixed-term lease and obtained before the lease is completed. Otherwise the order will be invalid and the lease will have the full protection of the Act unless the lease was conditional on the order being made; or unless the lease was regranted by endorsing the exclusion on it and referring to the court order (*Essexcrest Ltd* v *Evenlex Ltd* [1988] 1 EGLR 69; or the tenant was occupying as tenant at will pending the grant of the order.

The danger for the landlord, which he needs to avoid, is allowing continued occupation by the tenant after the expiry of the term where that tenancy is contracted out of the Act. If the landlord receives rent for any period following the expiry of the contractual term a new tenancy is created with security of tenure under the Act.

CHAPTER 12

Approach to negotiations

12.1 Checklists of key points

Landlords and tenants have different requirements of the same property and so approach negotiations with different objectives. From the landlord's point of view it is necessary to consider the value of his investment in the premises as a whole and, where relevant, as part of a larger portfolio. The lease may be an industrial unit contained within an estate, a single shop in an arcade or a single floor within a multi-tenanted office building: in each the market conditions affecting adjoining property will provide comparables.

The tenant's viewpoint will be more concerned with the future of its business and operating costs in that location and future flexibility.

12.2 The landlord's viewpoint

These are the issues the landlord will need to consider:

- Whether the building has become outdated and as a consequence whether the level of rent is falling.
- Whether there are future proposals for the area (adjoining development or local planning controls) which would change the area's character: either improve its attractiveness or otherwise.
- Whether the unit may be redeveloped/refurbished.
- Whether the timing of the other leases affect the current lease.
- Whether the landlord would be able to relet if the existing tenant vacated.

If, following consideration of the above points, the landlord chooses to offer the existing tenant a new lease then he may consider:

- Whether there are diminishing rental values owing to obsolescence.
- Whether the terms of the existing lease can be improved and thereby improve its investment value.
- Whether the letting area can be increased and whether the tenant

requires expansion space.
- Whether this is a good time to sort out the building or estate: swap or release land or open up potential income.
- Whether the landlord is happy with the tenant and, if not, whether there are grounds to oust him.
- Dilapidations.

CHAPTER 13

Position until renewal

13.1 Tactics while the lease continues

The basis on which the lease continues is simply stated: a tenancy which qualifies under the Act continues after the expiry of the contractual term until it is brought to an end under the Act. Until then the tenancy continues on the same terms and at the same rent as the contractual tenancy. This means that the landlord will have the same remedies available for a breach of the terms by way of forfeiture and/or for non-payment of rent by way of distress. Similarly, the tenant will be able to assign the lease so long as it complies with its terms in doing so.

However, if the tenant has ceased to qualify under the Act (for example because it has incorporated its business, but failed to assign the lease to it) then the landlord may bring the lease to an end by giving between three and six-month's notice under section 24(3). This will only be of tactical advantage to the landlord if it is able to relet the premises quickly and at a better rent; otherwise the better option may be to renegotiate with the tenant for a new lease to ensure a continuation of rent income from the premises.

Where the tenant still continues to qualify under the Act and it is entitled to renew its lease, the relevant tactics are when and how to initiate the renewal procedure (see later) and when it has been initiated whether to make tactical use of an interim rent application (see later also).

13.2 How the lease ends

While the tenant is entitled to continue at the premises on the same terms as the existing lease under section 24 of the Act, the contractual lease itself, will, in the case of a fixed term, end by effluxion of time and, in the case of a periodic tenancy, end by a tenant's notice to quit, but the contractual termination is still subject to the statutory continuation. These are common law methods by which the tenancy ends. In addition the tenancy can be brought to an end by both parties by surrender or by the landlord exercising the option to forfeit the lease. In the case of surrender or forfeiture the tenancy ends and there is no consequential right of renewal.

However, in all other cases the tenant has the right to continue at the premises under the Act and the position then is as follows:

- If following the expiry of the term or a notice to quit the tenant wishes to walk away from the premises then it must serve notice under section 27.
- If the landlord wants to initiate the renewal procedure then it must serve notice under section 25. The date of that notice will affect the start of the new lease, the commencement date for the new rent and any interim rent application (see later).
- If the tenant wants to initiate the renewal procedure then it must serve a request under section 26. This will also affect the start date for the new lease, rent and interim rent applications (see later).

Unless and until the relevant notice/request has been served the lease continues under section 24 of the Act even though the contractual term may have ended. The impact of this continuation on the original tenant and his liability for rent arrears was demonstrated in *City of London Corporation* v *Fell*; *Herbert Duncan Ltd* v *Cluttons* [1993] 04 EG 115.

CHAPTER 14

Rental valuation

The valuation date for the new rent is the date of the hearing. In negotiations, however, this date can be fixed by agreement, often corresponding to the expiry of the old lease. In depressed market conditions and with rental values falling, the tenant's tactic may be to delay this date until the completion of documentation. If the market changes and market values move up, tactics will be reversed.

If the court is required to fix the rent it will have regard to the terms of the lease and determine a rent which, on those terms, the property might reasonably be expected to be let in the open market by a willing lessor. The rent is arguably therefore the last thing to be negotiated until all of the other terms are clear. However, in practice it is usually the first thing to be agreed: other terms are then negotiated around it.

The rent is difficult to establish in a depressed market because there are financial incentives which landlords will offer to attract tenants. This also makes comparables unreliable. Rent-free periods can be difficult to analyse accurately. However, it is the incentives such as reverse premiums, fitting-out work and even the buying-in of old leases on other properties, that cause severe difficulty in establishing the open market rental value.

Landlords giving generous incentives have over the last few years turned to confidentiality clauses in an attempt to suppress information that could potentially damage their investment interest. This additional hurdle can further frustrate the already difficult job of identifying true comparable evidence.

If the court settles the rent there are certain matters which are disregarded in the valuation and set out in section 34 of the Act. These are dealt with below.

14.1 Tenant's occupation

The court is required to disregard any damage or alterations (not improvements) to the premises by the tenant: effectively it will assume that the premises are in the state of repair postulated by the lease and assume that the tenant had never been there. This may have an effect on the user if the tenant obtained a personal planning permission or established the user of the premises by being in occupation prior to January 1 1964.

14.2 Tenant's goodwill
There is no clear definition of goodwill for these purposes, but it does not cover that element of the property which would attract customers merely because of the position of the property (ie location and goodwill) and not attributable to the tenant in occupation.

14.3 Improvements carried out by the tenant
That is, otherwise than in pursuance of an obligation to the landlord, either during the current tenancy or completed not more than 21 years before the new tenancy application – the timing of a section 25 notice can therefore have a significant impact. It should be remembered that alterations by the tenant or his predecessors do not automatically constitute improvement and, in some cases, can have a downward effect on value.

14.4 Disregard any effect on rent as a result of a licence belonging to the tenant
This has particular relevance to licenced premises which are no longer excluded following the Landlord and Tenant (Licenced Premises) Act 1990. However, it would be fair to say that regard would be had to the likelihood of another tenant obtaining a licence.

CHAPTER 15

Renewal procedure

There are advantages from tactical use of the procedure for renewing the lease, especially where either landlord or tenant fail to follow the procedure properly. For the tenant the wrong result can be fatal: a loss of the right to renew the lease. However the landlord can also be caught out by tactical use of the section 26 request and its effects on interim rent applications.

15.1 Section 25 notice tactics

The relevant tactic here for the landlord arises where the landlord is opposing renewal under section 30(1)(e), (f) or (g) of the Act. The tactic is to quote another ground in the section 25 notice. The reason is that if the tenant then claims disturbance compensation it will have to show that it would have been able to resist the other ground before succeeding in its claim. However, the landlord must be aware that any grounds stated have to be genuine. If the section 25 notice gives a false or incorrect ground then it will be wholly invalid even though the other grounds are correct.

The section 25 notice has to be in the form prescribed by the Act and cover the whole of the property in the tenancy. The section 25 notice also has to set out an end date for the tenancy: this cannot be earlier than the date on which the fixed term tenancy would have expired by effluxion of time or in the case of a periodic tenancy the earliest date on which the landlord might have brought it to an end by notice to quit. The section 25 notice gives the tenant two months to tell the landlord in writing whether it is willing to give up possession on the end date; and it further states whether the landlord intends to oppose the tenant's right to renew and if so on which grounds under section 30 of the Act: see earlier comments on the tactic of quoting more than one ground.

The section 25 notice can only be served not more than 12 nor less than six months before the end date specified in it. This means that if the landlord fails to serve notice by the date on which the contractual tenancy would have otherwise ended it can still do so providing the notice then specifies a later end date and is served within the period of 12 to six months before that date. The landlord also has to make sure that the notice includes his name and address – see *Pearson* v *Alyo* [1990] 1 EGLR 114 and clearly describes the premises – *Herongrove Ltd* v *Wates City of London Properties plc* [1988] 1 EGLR 82 otherwise it will be invalid.

The tenant has two months in which to serve the counternotice to the section 25 notice. The tenant has to make application to the court for a new lease not less than two nor more than four months after the section 25 notice has been given to the tenants. If the counternotice and the court application are not made then the tenant's right of renewal under the Act is lost. The court has no power to extend these time-limits.

15.2 Section 26 request tactics

The issue here is whether the tenant can make tactical use of its right to initiate the renewal procedure by serving the section 26 request and the landlord needs to be aware of the tactics the tenant is considering.

The position is as follows:

- If no section 26 request is served on the landlord then, provided the landlord does not serve a section 25 notice, the lease will continue which for the tenant means rent at the old level under the old lease. This will continue until the landlord initiates the renewal procedure by means of a section 25 notice. The landlord may forget to do this or in a falling market deliberately avoid doing so perhaps with the expectation that the market may pick up, which would then be an appropriate time for the landlord to initiate the renewal procedure.
- If the tenant needs a new lease and new level of rent, perhaps to assign the lease or to fix the rent because the market levels are likely to rise, then it would be commercially tactical to initiate the renewal procedure with a section 26 request.
- If no section 25 notice has been served by the landlord and it has been landlord for just less than five years, then the tenant should consider whether the landlord is deliberately delaying service of the section 25 notice in order to qualify under the opposition ground in section 30(1)(*g*). This is the ground that allows a landlord to oppose renewal because at the end of the current tenancy the landlord intends to occupy the premises for the

purpose or partly for the purpose of a business to be carried on by it or in the case of an individual as its residence. The five-year period has to end with the end date in the section 25 notice or section 26 request. The tenant can therefore break that qualifying period by initiating the renewal procedure and serving a section 26 request.

- If rents are rising or likely to rise and the landlord has not served a section 25 notice, then the tenant should consider whether it would be tactical to serve the section 26 request in order to gain up to six months at the level of rent in the old lease. This is because the tenant can state in the section 26 request a start date for the new lease which is up to 12 months ahead of the date of the section 26 request (although it may not be earlier than the date on which the contractual tenancy would have otherwise ended). The effect will be that the landlord will then be unable to serve a section 25 notice and the old tenancy will continue at the old level of rent until the start date set out in the section 26 request; and the landlord will be prevented from claiming interim rent until after that new start date.

The section 26 request, like the section 25 notice, has to be in the form prescribed by the Act and, as described, has to set out the date on which the new lease is to start which may not be earlier than the date on which the tenancy would have otherwise ended. However the section 26 request must be served on the landlord at least six but not more than 12 months before the new start date and otherwise has to make clear what the tenant proposes in respect of rent, term and other conditions for the new lease.

15.3 Tactical use of interim-rent applications

Interim rents were introduced to prevent tenants procrastinating at the end of their leases and then walking away. Even if a landlord served his section 25 notice at the earliest possible date, the delays inherent in the judicial system often give rise to a delay between the lease termination date and the court hearing.

In *Charles Follet Ltd* v *Cabtell Investments Ltd* [1987] 2 EGLR 88 the Court of Appeal noted "tenants in times of inflation, could readily spin out the steps prescribed by the 1954 Act and the rules of court so as unfairly to prolong the continuation of the old rent under section 24".

To redress this the Law of Property Act 1969 introduced section

24A to the 1954 Act. This enabled the landlord to apply to the court to determine an interim rent during the statutory continuation of the tenancy.

The date for assessing the interim rent is the later of:

- the date of service of the interim rent application, or;
- the date specified in the landlord's section 25 Notice or the tenant's section 26 request.

An interim rent is determined having regard to the terms and conditions of the existing lease and as required by section 34(1) and (2) of the Act, but on the assumption of a new annual tenancy being granted from the date of valuation.

Standard practice by both the courts and surveyors has been to agree the new lease rent and to fix the interim rent by adjusting the new fixed term rent downwards to reflect the "perceived" disadvantage of an annual tenancy. At least this is how the section has been interpreted since its inception in 1969 over the last 20-odd years of what has broadly been a continually rising property market. Subject to local and regional variances, a discount or "rental cushion" of 10% or 15% has been applied.

During times of recession when fixed-term leases can be perceived as a millstone, it may be argued that a tenancy from year to year is more valuable in rent terms than a fixed-term tenancy. In today's market, there may be little or no incentive for the landlord to make a section 24A application. If he does not, the tenant cannot make an interim rent application to reduce his rent burden.

Positions have reversed and it can often be the landlord who has to weigh up the benefit of maintaining the existing rental income stream by delaying proceedings against the possibility of a reduced rent being determined at a later court hearing. However, changes may be imminent and the Law Commission has recommended that tenants may make interim rent applications and has further recommended the removal of the "cushion" effect: see Chapter 18.3. A practical example of the court determining both final rent and interim rent is shown in *French* v *Commercial Union Life Assurance Co plc* [1993] 24 EG 115.

15.4 Tenant's court application

When
The tenant's application must be made in the period of two to four

months after the section 25 notice is served or the section 26 request is sent. This is regardless of how negotiations are proceeding. If the tenant fails to protect his renewal rights, he will lose his negotiating position and possibly the lease. There may be some scope for making a late court application but this is very limited: see *Ward-Lee* v *Linehan* [1993] 20 EG 125.

If the landlord then agrees to renew it will be on open market terms and possibly at a higher rent.

What happens next
Terms are often agreed and a court hearing is not needed to settle the lease. Where it is, the court will not necessarily settle all the terms from scratch. Instead the usual directions for trial will provide for the landlord to submit to the tenant a draft lease upon which the tenant replies with a list of those terms to which it objects. This will then narrow the issues between the parties. Both parties will then exchange expert's reports as to terms and comparables on rent. If settlement still cannot be reached at that stage the court effectively settles the outstanding issues and the start of the lease will be fixed at three months after the tenants application is disposed of.

Where the tenant wishes to vacate the premises and therefore does not wish to negotiate new terms it would still be tactical to follow the renewal procedure and protect its renewal rights by making the court application. This provides it with an opportunity to negotiate a convenient vacation date. Where the tenant fails to make the court application it will still need to serve notice under section 27 to bring the tenancy to an end otherwise the tenant will remain liable for the rent under the lease and for any breach of its terms.

CHAPTER 16

Key terms of the renewed lease

The court will, if required, determine the terms of the new lease and in doing so will have regard to the terms of the existing lease and current market practice.

16.1 Term

While the court is limited to granting a maximum term of 14 years, it is possible to obtain by agreement any length of term, but these usually range from between the institutional 25 years to a short period of one or two years where grounds for possession could ultimately be proven. In uncertain markets, tenants seek shorter terms and it is then the landlords who encourage tenants to accept longer periods.

The position is set out in section 33 of the Act. The court has to order such term as is reasonable in all the circumstances. However, the court will consider the term under the existing lease (*Betty's Cafés Ltd* v *Phillips Furnishing Stores Ltd* [1959] AC 20 and the period during which the tenant has been holding over – *London & Provincial Millinery Stores Ltd* v *Barclays Bank Ltd* [1962] 1 WLR 510. Where the landlord wants to develop, but it is unable to prove ground (*f*) under section 30 of the Act the court may grant a landlords break clause: *Becker* v *Hill Street Properties Ltd* [1990] 2 EGLR 78.

16.2 Rent review cycle and rent

Older leases often reflect a lack of appreciation of the inflation markets subsequently experienced. As a result, rent reviews are spaced at seven-year intervals or, in some cases, 14-year intervals. The court can be persuaded by market practice, but having regard to section 34(3) of the Act the court will also look at the existing lease and its terms of rent review: *JH Edwards & Sons Ltd* v *Central London Commercial Estates Ltd* (1983) 271 EG 697 and *Stylo Shoes Ltd* v *Manchester Royal Exchange Ltd* (1967) 204 EG 803. However, the rent review cycle will have an effect on the level of rent and both should be considered at the same time.

The level of rent is dictated by the terms of section 34 (see earlier) although the other terms of the lease will impact on the rent: see *O'May* v *City of London Real Property Co Ltd* v (1983) 261 EG 1185.

16.3 Repairs
The liability imposed on the tenant for repair tends to be dictated by the type of property in question; however, it is common for industrial estates/out of town offices to include an obligation for the landscaping, courtyards, paved areas etc, retained by the landlord's managing company, the cost being recouped through the service charge.

16.4 Alienation
The tenant may consider the future of his occupation in the property and seek to obtain as much flexibility as possible. The landlord will wish to allow as much flexibility as is necessary to obtain the best rent, but retaining the ability to manage the estate/building properly.

16.5 Break clause
Thinking ahead the landlord may wish to see a break clause inserted on the grounds that he either wishes to redevelop the property or intends to occupy it for his own business, although this will be a matter of negotiation.

16.6 Other terms
Dependent on the circumstances of each individual property and landlord and tenant, other terms will come into play, but now is the time to ensure they are covered to avoid further expense and inconvenience and preferably without leaving it to the court to settle the terms. The court has limited ability to change the other terms of the lease except by having regard to the existing lease and relevant circumstances under section 35 of the Act. It will tend to follow the existing lease unless there are good reasons to do otherwise: *Cardshops Ltd* v *Davies* [1971] 1 WLR 579.

CHAPTER 17

Opposition to renewal

Reference has been made before to the landlords tactic of quoting more than one ground for opposing renewal in the section 25 notice when using grounds (*f*) and (*g*). However, the landlord must also consider whether his circumstances genuinely fit the grounds and this is now dealt with.

17.1 The relevant grounds

The landlord may oppose the tenant's application for a new tenancy on the grounds in section 30(1) of the Act. The landlord has to specify the ground in the section 25 notice or in the reply to the tenant's section 26 request. There are a total of seven grounds but the most common and commercially relevant are ground (*f*) demolition or reconstruction of premises and ground (*g*) where the landlord intends to use the premises for his own use.

17.2 Ground (*a*)

The landlord opposes renewal here because the tenant ought not to be granted a new tenancy in view of the state of repair of the premises, resulting from the tenant's failure to comply with the his repairing obligations.

However, forfeiture and the conditions for relief are possibly more effective.

The landlord should consider what he wants. If he wants possession then he should oppose the new tenancy under ground (*a*). The tenant may obtain relief from forfeiture and that will hold up renewal. If the object is to complete the work then he should seek forfeiture.

17.3 Ground (*b*)

The landlord opposes renewal because of the tenant's persistent delay in paying rent.

To show this the landlord must demonstrate what rent fell due and when; and also when it was paid the length of delay and any steps taken for recovery: see *Hopcutt* v *Carver* (1969) 209 EG 1069.

17.4 Ground (c)

The landlord opposes renewal here because there are other substantial breaches of the lease or other reasons connected with the tenants use or management of the premises.

This does not have to involve breaches of obligations to the landlord, but may be breaches of law generally.

Turner & Bell v *Searles* (1977) 33 P&CR 208 – proposed use in breach of planning control; and *Beard* v *Williams* [1986] 1 EGLR 148 – illegal siting of caravan.

17.5 Ground (d)

The landlord opposes renewal here because there is suitable alternative accommodation on offer.

However he will need to show:

- That the terms are reasonable having regard to the terms of the current tenancy and other relevant circumstances.
- That the accommodation is suitable for the tenant's requirements (including preserving goodwill) having regard to nature and class of his business and the situation and extent of and facilities afforded by the premises.
- That the time at which it is available is also suitable.
- That the landlord has offered and is willing to provide or secure the provision of it.

The problem is that the offer must have been made before the service of the section 25 notice and still be on offer at the date of the hearing.

17.6 Ground (e)

The landlord oppose renewal here because the tenant is a sub-tenant of part and the landlord can show:

- That the aggregate of rents for the premises and remainder of the property is less than for letting as a whole.
- That the landlord requires possession for the purpose of letting or otherwise disposing of the whole.
- That the tenant ought not accordingly to be granted new tenancy.

17.7 Ground (f)

The landlord opposes renewal here because at the end of the tenancy the landlord intends to demolish or reconstruct the premises or a substantial part of it or to carry out substantial work of construction on it or part of it, and he cannot reasonably do so without obtaining possession of the premises.

Showing a genuine intention
These are the key points:

- The landlord's intention has to be more than a mere hope: it must be firm and settled and have a reasonable prospect of success: *Edwards* v *Thompson* [1990] 2 EGLR 71.
- The landlord's intention is such that a reasonable man could not reach any other conclusion than that of the landlord in the likely prospect of his plans being achieved: *Capocci* v *Goble* [1987] 2 EGLR 102.
- The landlord's intention must be proved as at the date of the hearing: *Betty's Cafés Ltd* v *Phillips Furnishings Stores Ltd* [1959] AC 20.

Showing there will be demolition or reconstruction
This depends on the extent of demolition in each case and the difference between the premises before and after the works. The issue is whether these works involve the demolition or reconstruction of a substantial part of the premises or the carrying out of a substantial work of construction on them: *Romulus Trading Co Ltd* v *Henry Smith's Charity Trustees* [1990] 2 EGLR 75 and also *Graysim Holdings Ltd* v *P&O Property Holdings Ltd* [1993] 05 EG 141.

Showing that possession is required
The landlord has to show that he could not reasonably demolish or reconstruct the premises without having possession. However, this requirement has to be understood in the context of section 31A of the Act. This effectively provides that the landlord is deemed unable to show that he requires possession if either of the following apply:

- That the tenant is prepared to agree a new lease which will include provisions for the landlord to have access in order to carry out the proposed works and that, on that basis, the landlord can complete its works without possession or interfering to a substantial extent or for a substantial time with the use of the premises for the business carried on by the tenant.
- Or, the tenant is prepared to accept a tenancy of an economically separable part of the premises and either the point set out in the preceding paragraph is satisfied or the landlord, being able to

possess the remainder of the premises, will be able to carry out the work.

It is suggested that the terms of section 31A are specifically checked to see that they apply to the premises concerned but, in principle, this raises the following tactics for the tenant of which the landlord should be aware:

- The burden of proving opposition to the new lease under ground (f) falls on the landlord.
- If the landlord has sufficient evidence to prove ground (f) the tenant can then place a further burden on the landlord to show that possession of the whole of the premises is needed to carry out the works where the tenant is prepared to agree to either section 31A (a) or (b).

Where the landlord fails to show that possession is needed to the whole premises then the tenant will be entitled to a new tenancy on the following basis:

- A new lease of the whole of the premises which include provisions for access by the landlord to carry out the works.
- Or, a new lease of an economically separable part of the premises on the terms set out above.

Showing when the works are to be carried out
The works must be proposed to be carried out within a reasonable time after the end of the lease allowing for the holding over under section 24 of the Act.

Tenant's defences
Given what the landlord has to show in order to establish ground (f), the landlord needs to be aware that there will be a number of defences available to the tenant and prepare accordingly.

These are the tenants defences:

- That work to parts of the building which are not included in the lease to the tenant do not count against that tenant for the purposes of establishing this ground.
- That the works do not qualify as works of reconstruction, construction or demolition: see *Romulus Trading* v *Henry Smith Charity* [1990] 2 EGLR 75 and *Barth* v *Pritchard* [1990] 1 EGLR 109.
- That the works are not substantial enough to qualify for this

ground: see *Botterill* v *Bedfordshire County Council* [1985] 1 EGLR 82 and *Barth* v *Pritchard* [1990] 1 EGLR 109.
- That the landlord has the power of entry in the lease to carry out the works to the premises so that possession is unnecessary: see *Heath* v *Drown* [1973] AC 498.
- That the tenant is willing to agree to terms which would comply with section 31(A) of the Act: see above notes and also *Cerex Jewels Ltd* v *Peachey Property Corporation plc* [1986] 2 EGLR 65 and *Price* v *Esso Petroleum* (1980) 255 EG 243.

17.8 Ground (g)

The landlord opposes renewal here because at the end of the tenancy it intends to occupy the premises for the purposes, or partly for the purposes, of a business to be carried on by him there, or as his residence.

However, under section 30(2) the landlord cannot rely on this ground:

- If it acquired the premises within the five years of the end date in the section 25 notice or section 26 request.
- If between that acquisition and that end date there has been a tenancy or succession of them to which the Act applies.

There is some flexibility here as to the nature of the occupation which the landlord needs to establish to satisfy this ground:

- The occupation may be by a company in which the landlord has a controlling interest under section 30(3).
- The occupation may be by an agent or manager rather than the landlord directly as in *Skeet* v *Powell-Shetton* [1988] 2 EGLR 112.
- The occupation may be in premises which are not the same as those occupied by the tenant, but renewed or altered as in *Cam Gears Ltd* v *Cunningham* (1981) 258 EG 749.

CHAPTER 18

Rules on compensation

18.1 For disturbance

Under the Act the tenant can claim compensation for disturbance where the landlord successfully opposes his application for a new tenancy on grounds (e), (f) or (g) (Section 37). It is also payable where those grounds are shown in the section 25 notice or in the counternotice to the tenant's section 26 request and the tenant makes no application to the court, or subsequently withdraws any that has been made.

The landlord's tactic here if there are other genuine grounds is to include them in the section 25 notice or in the counternotice to the tenant's section 26 request so that the tenant will be required to show that it would have successfully been able to oppose those other grounds in order to succeed in his claim for compensation for disturbance.

The amount of compensation is calculated in accordance with the Landlord and Tenant Act 1954 (Appropriate Multiplier) Order 1990 and the Local Government and Housing Act 1989 as follows:

- Where the section 25 notice or counternotice to the section 26 request is served before April 1 1990, it is 3 x old rateable value, but doubled if the tenant has used the premises for business purposes for more than 14 years.
- Where this is on or after April 1 1990 it is 1 x the new rateable value, but doubled if the same 14 year rule applies.

There are provisions in the 1990 order and 1989 Act which apply if:
- The tenancy was completed before April 1 1990 or pursuant to a pre-April 1990 contract.
- The section 25 notice or counternotice to the tenant's section 26 request is made before April 2000.

In these circumstances the tenant can by notice elect that compensation is assessed under section 37 with the rateable value set at March 31 1990. The amount is then 8 x old rateable value (or 16 x old rateable value if the 14-year rule applies).

The Landlord and Tenant Act 1954 (Appropriate Multiplier) Order 1990 when read in conjunction with the Local Government and Housing Act 1989 section 149 and Schedule 7 provides as follows:

- Where the landlord's notice or his reply to the tenant's request was served before April 1 1990, compensation is on the old basis, ie 3 x old rateable value (or 6 x old rateable value if the 14-year rule is satisfied).
- Where the relevant date is on or after April 1 1990 compensation is 1 x new rateable value (or 2 x new rateable value if the 14-year rule is satisfied).
- Where any part of the "holding" comprises "domestic property" such as where a tenant resides in the flat above his shop special provisions apply as set out below.

If the landlord's section 25 notice or the tenant's section 26 request is given after April 1 1990 then any part of the "holding" which comprises "domestic property" is disregarded for the purposes of section 37(5). The disturbance compensation is based only on the value of the business part of the property; but the tenant is entitled to a "sum equal to his reasonable expenses in removing from the domestic property" where he occupied the whole or any part of the domestic property on the date the landlord gave the notice or the reply to the request. Disputes over the removal expenses are determined by the court.

The transitional arrangements apply where:

- The tenancy was entered into before April 1 1990 or was entered into on or after that date and in pursuance of a pre-April 1 1990 contract.
- The landlord's notice or his reply to the request is given before April 1 2000.

If these provisions apply the tenant may by notice to the landlord elect (not less than two months and not more than four months after the landlord's notice or the tenant's request is served ie during the period in which any application for a new tenancy would have to be made). That compensation is assessed for the entire holding on the old section 37 basis, but with the date for determining rateable value set at March 31 1990. Where the tenant makes this election the multiplier is 8 x old rateable value (or 16 x old rateable value if the 14-year rule is satisfied).

18.2 For improvements

The Landlord and Tenant Act 1927 sections 1 to 17 and Part III of the 1954 Act provide for compensation for improvements which add to the letting value of the premises at the end of the lease.

To claim compensation under section 3 of the 1927 Act the tenant must have complied fully with the registration procedure when the improvements were first made:

- The tenant serves notice of intention to carry out the improvements with specifications and plans of the works.
- The landlord then has three months to object by notice. If not, the tenant can proceed with the works. If so, the tenant can apply to court to certify the improvement complies with the Act. This will not be certified if the landlord has offered to carry out the improvement in return for a reasonable increase in rent; nor if the work has been completed before the court deals with it.
- The increase in the value of the premises as a direct result of the works.
- Or, the reasonable cost of carrying out the same when the tenancy ends less the cost (if any) of putting the works into a state of repair, excluding such cost covered by the tenants liability to repair the premises.

This is set out in more detail in section 1(2) of the 1927 Act, but its terms are such that the tenant's claim may not be worth pursuing.

18.3 Reform

The Law Commission has reported on the 1954 Act and made some far-reaching proposals for change: see Law Commission Paper no 208, 1992.

A summary of the key proposals is set out below.

The extent of the Act
The extent of the Act is to be changed as follows:

- Types of cccupation.
  A tenant will qualify for protection and a landlord able to oppose renewal, however the business is structured. This means a tenant will be protected if he has a controlling interest in the company that runs the business and a landlord will be similarly entitled to oppose renewal.

- Excluding the Act.
  There will be no need for prior court approval. Instead, the clause excluding the Act will be endorsed on or contained in the lease in a statutory prescribed format.
  Agreements to surrender where the tenant has been in occupation under the tenancy for less than one month will have the same formal requirements.
  Agreements to surrender entered into after that period will be free from statutory restrictions.

Statutory procedure
The procedures under the Act will also be changed as follows:

- Section 40 notices.
  These will be extended with provision that a failure to respond results in liability for breach of statutory duty.
- Tenant's counternotice.
  The provisions for counternotice will be repealed.
- Court applications.
  Both parties will be able to apply to court without the need for the usual two month period to expire.
  The latest date by which applications must be made will be the termination date in the notice. The parties may also agree extensions; but any extensions of time must be agreed before an existing time-limit has expired.

Interim rent
On interim rent:

- Who can apply.
  It is proposed that either party can apply for interim rent.
- From when is it payable.
  It is proposed that interim rent will be payable from the earliest date that might be specified in the statutory notice, where the other party that has not served the notice is applying for it; otherwise it will be payable from the date in the statutory notice.
- How much?
  If the renewal is not opposed by the landlord, and the tenancy is granted, the interim rent will be equal to the rent payable under that tenancy; this will effectively back-date the new rent to the date specified in the statutory notice; otherwise the current rules will continue to apply.

TENANT FAILURE

CHAPTER 19

Previous tenants and guarantors

19.1 Possible action by the landlord

Where a tenant has defaulted either in paying rent or in complying with the terms of the lease, the landlord needs to consider whether he can bring an action against any earlier tenants and guarantors if, for some reason (perhaps insolvency), the current tenant is not worth pursuing.

The landlord can bring an action against previous tenants and guarantors in the following circumstances:

- The tenant or guarantor is the original tenant or original guarantor named in the original lease.
- The previous tenant or guarantor (being an intermediate tenant or guarantor) has covenanted directly with the landlord in a licence to assign to observe and perform the terms and conditions in the lease for the remainder of its term.

This emphasises the need to ensure that where there is an assignment by a tenant the landlord gives consent by a formal licence to assign. The same applies to any intermediate guarantor.

If there is no formal licence to assign with such provision then the intermediate tenants and guarantors cease to be liable to the landlord for any breach of the terms of the lease when the intermediate tenant (and its respective guarantor) part with possession of the premises.

19.2 The original tenant/guarantors

The position of the original tenant and guarantor in the context of the insolvency of a subsequent tenant is as follows:

- The original tenant remains liable throughout the period of the lease even though it is assigned.
- The original guarantor of an original tenant is similarly liable to the original landlord unless his guarantee is expressly limited to exclude liability once the original tenant has assigned the lease.

Thus, a guarantor's obligation to accept a new lease replacing a lease disclaimed on behalf of an insolvent tenant will similarly out-live an assignment of the lease unless there is express wording to the contrary: *Coronation Street Industrial Properties Ltd* v *Ingall Industries plc* [1989] 1 EGLR 86.

The position of the original tenant and his guarantors has been considered by the Law Commission (report number 174, 1988) whose recommendations, if implemented, alter the liability of the original tenant, subsequent assignees and guarantors of each. The effect of such recommendations will be as follows:

- That the liability of the original tenant will end when the lease is assigned.
- That the liability of an intermediate tenant will similarly end on assignment of the lease.
- That the liability of a guarantor of either original or intermediate tenant will cease when the party whose liabilities it has guaranteed stopped being the tenant.

However, until the law is changed the original tenant, intermediate tenant and guarantor's liability remain a valuable source of recourse by the landlord for non-payment of rent or default in the terms of the lease by the current tenant.

The original tenant

The original tenant is liable throughout the term for all covenants in the lease by privity of contract unless released or unless the lease provides otherwise: *Warnford Investments Ltd* v *Duckworth* [1979] Ch 127. This means that the original tenant is liable even after it has assigned the lease and that liability includes increases in rent and any interest due to the landlord. The original tenant is liable for such matters from the due date and not from date of demand.

There is no duty on the landlord to mitigate his loss. So the original tenant is still liable even if there is a delay by the landlord in making the demand.

A landlord also owes no duty of care to an original tenant to ensure that subsequent assignees have sufficient financial status to meet the rent and other obligations in the lease. The landlord need not pursue his alternative options (if any) first but can go straight for the original tenant: *Norwich Union Life Insurance Society* v *Low Profile Fashions* [1992] 1 EGLR 86.

However, the original tenant (and intermediate tenants) will have the benefit (if any) of indemnities from subsequent tenants as follows:

- Under section 77 of the Law of Property Act 1925 or section 24(1)(*b*) of the Land Registration Act 1925 by way of an implied indemnity from the immediate assignee where assignment was for value.
- And, under any rights to contribution in quasi contract by *Moule v Garrett* (1872) LR 7 Exch 101.

However, the original tenant is not entitled either to distrain against the current tenants goods to make good sums he is called upon by the landlord to repay nor is he entitled to call for a reassignment to him of the lease.

The original tenant may nevertheless seek to reduce his liability by providing a default option in the assignment. This, in effect, is a provision in the assignment of the lease by the original tenant for reassignment of the lease in the event of default by the assignee. Such a default option will provide that if at any time during the term the original tenant is called upon to make good default by the assignee, or any other person in whom the premises are then vested, or pays damages or costs as a result of such default, or has to indemnify any person against the consequences of that default; then the original tenant may serve notice on the assignee requiring it to reassign to the original tenant the unexpired residue of the term granted by the lease. The default option should also impose obligations on the assignee to pass on similar provisions on any subsequent assignment.

The original tenant may also have claims against defaulting tenants' guarantors on the basis of subrogation: *Kumar v Dunning* [1987] 2 EGLR 39 and *Selous Street Properties v Oronel Fabrics Ltd* (1984) 270 EG 643.

The intermediate tenant

The intermediate tenant's liability is based on privity of estate. Once the intermediate tenant has assigned the lease he is only liable to the landlord for future breaches where he has given direct covenants in a licence to assign; but such liability under those direct covenants will (subject to the wording of the covenant) last for the whole term of the lease even after it has assigned. Moreover, there is a possibility that suing on direct covenants in a licence to assign may not waive the landlord's right to forfeit *London & County (A & D) Ltd v Wilfred Sportman Ltd* [1971] Ch 764.

Current tenant

The assignment of a lease (even an oral tenancy) must be by deed for privity of estate to be created. The current tenant is liable while tenant and subsequently following further assignment as an intermediate tenant, but a tenant is not liable for arrears of rent due under the lease before the assignment to it or for once and for all breaches of covenant committed before the assignment to it: *Parry v Robinson-Wyllie Ltd* [1987] 2 EGLR 133.

When arrears of rent arising following a rent review become ascertained during the period in which the term was vested in an assignee, but relate to a period before the term was vested in it, then, in the absence of clear agreement to the contrary the assignee is not liable to the landlord to pay those arrears. Also under privity of estate, assignees are only liable for covenants that "touch and concern" the land and not personal covenants, eg non-competition covenants. This can be remedied by obtaining direct covenants from the assignee to observe and perform all covenants in the lease.

Guarantors

The guarantors' obligations rest entirely on their contractual covenant. Therefore, the wording is critical, eg a guarantee of rent "during the term of the lease" ends with the contractual term and does not continue into any statutory extension: *Junction Estates Ltd v Cope* (1974) 27 P&CR 482.

This should be contrasted with the case where the phrase "tenancy created by the lease" did continue the guarantors liability into the statutory extension: see *GMS Syndicate v Gary Elliot Ltd* (1980) 258 EG 251.

Moreover, a guarantors' liability for pre-existing arrears (or breaches of covenant) survive a surrender or forfeiture and can include an outstanding rent review: *Torminster Properties Ltd v Green* (1983) 267 EG 256.

However, the liability of a guarantor does survive a disclaimer of the lease by the current tenant's liquidator. The liquidated tenant's guarantor is released by disclaimer. In a modern surety clause there is likely to be a primary obligation on the guarantor to take a new lease on disclaimer. That obligation continues and the court will treat this as an enforceable agreement for lease even if the guarantor fails to complete the new lease. Further the benefit of a guarantee does run with the reversion (because it "touches and concerns" the land) in the absence of words to the contrary: *Kumar v Dunning*. The issue of disclaimer is dealt with further below.

A guarantor's liability will not be affected by a rent review (even if he was not a party to negotiations) but, unless the guarantors covenant provides otherwise, the guarantor will be released by a variation in the terms of the lease or any forbearance given to the tenant, eg surrender of part will release guarantors. The landlord should check whether there are guarantors who could be released by variations or forbearance (either of the current tenant or prior tenants) before agreeing to variation and obtaining their consent.

19.3 Other interested parties
Where a landlord assigns interest
The position changes when the reversion, the landlord's interest, has been assigned by the landlord. Payment of rent to a former landlord before the tenant has notice of the change is good payment so it is essential for a new landlord to ensure that notice of the sale of the reversion is given to all tenants on the purchase of an investment property.

The right to sue for rent arrears accrued prior to the sale of the reversion (or for other breaches by the tenant) passes from the seller of the reversion to the buyer under section 141(1) of the Law of Property Act 1925.

This is confirmed in respect of rent by *London & County (A & D) Ltd v Wilfred Sportman Ltd* and in respect of breaches of other covenants by *Re King* [1963] Ch 459.

Although the benefit of a guarantee runs with the reversion as previously mentioned the benefit of a rent deposit will not automatically pass and in the absence of express provisions to the contrary the original landlord may not be entitled to pass it to the purchaser of the reversion.

Subtenants
There is no privity of estate between headlandlord and subtenant. Consequently a subtenant has no direct liability to the headlandlord on the headlease or the sublease covenants save for restrictive covenants of which he has notice. However, headlandlords often require direct covenants to perform the headlease covenants, covered by a formal licence to sublet and this creates privity of contract.

If the headlease is forfeited, the sublease will end as well, but the subtenant can apply for relief from forfeiture. The court is likely to order the subtenant to accept a lease in the same terms as the headlease even if different from those of the sublease. Moreover a subtenant of part where the subtenant occupies part of the premises comprised in the headlease.

If the headlease is surrendered the sublease survives by section 139(1) of the Law of Property Act 1925, but disclaimer of the headlease determines a sublease although the subtenant may obtain a vesting order.

Under section 6 Law of Distress Amendment Act 1908 there are special provisions where there is non payment of rent by the headtenant. The headlandlord can serve notice on a lawful subtenant requiring payment of the subtenant's rent direct to the headlandlord until the intermediate landlord's arrears are cleared. The service of the notice creates a relationship of landlord and tenant between headlandlord and the subtenant. This right is unaffected by the appointment of an administrative receiver, ie the landlord takes priority. In *Rhodes* v *Allied Dunbar (Pension Services) Ltd* [1989] 1 EGLR 78 the receivers of the intermediate tenant were not entitled to distrain against a subtenant who was paying their rent direct to the head landlord by virtue of section 6.

A subtenant holding over under the statutory continuation in the Landlord and Tenant Act 1954 after the expiry of the headlease becomes the direct tenant of the headlandlord who can enforce the sublease covenants against him: section 65(2) Landlord and Tenant Act 1954.

19.4 Reform: privity of contract

The position of the original tenant/guarantor and the doctrine of privity of contract have been reviewed in Chapters 3 and 8; it must also be considered in terms of the report of the Law Commission (report no 174, 1988) – *Landlord and Tenant Law, Privity of Contract and Estate*.

In a statement on March 31 1993, the Lord Chancellor announced that the Government intended to adopt the Law Commission's proposals on extinguishing the doctrine of privity of contract in leases. However, these proposals would be implemented for future, but not for existing, leases. The legislation would not be retrospective. Moreover, any changes in the law would not affect contracts entered into before the commencement of any new legislation.

The following notes discuss the contents and effects of such legislation given the terms of the draft rules attached to the Law Commissioners' report.

Tenant's position
The proposed new rule is that a tenant who assigns its lease will cease to be liable, on assignment, to comply with its terms including such covenants as to pay rent and to repair the premises.

This new rule will apply equally to original and intermediate tenants. The benefits and burdens of the lease will be taken on by the new tenant, and the old tenant together with his guarantor will be released from all liabilities under the lease. However, a former tenant or his guarantor will remain liabile for breaches of covenant taking place before the date of the assignment.

It is proposed that where there is a qualified alienation covenant (ie not to assign without landlord's consent) landlords may require that the old tenant guarantees the performance and observance of the terms of the lease by the new tenant. However, it is arguable that this would only be likely to succeed where it would be reasonable to impose such a condition under the Landlord and Tenant Act 1988. This is suggested by section 1(5) of the Landlord and Tenant Act 1988 because, under that section, it is reasonable for the landlord not to give approval where, if he withheld his consent and the tenant completed the assignment, the tenant would be in breach of covenant.

Guarantor's position
Guarantors under similar obligations to the landlord as those of the original tenant will also be released. It is arguable that a landlord might reasonably require as part of the licence to assign that the old guarantor joins with the old tenant in the guarantee of the performance and observance of the terms of the lease by the new tenant. It may help the landlord to include such a requirement in the alienation provisions of the lease.

Landlord's position
A new rule in similar terms to that for the tenant, will apply to the landlord. If the landlord assigns his reversion to a lease, he will released from any liability to perform his landlord's covenants, which usually include, among others, the repair and maintenance of common parts and the insurance of the premises.

However, the landlord's release is neither immediate nor automatic. The landlord will be required to give prior notice to the tenant. This notice will be in a prescribed form. The tenant will then have an opportunity to object to the release. If the terms of the release cannot be settled by agreement then there is provision for the matter to be determined by the court. If the tenant does object within the time fixed by the proposed new rules, then the landlord will be released from his covenants in the lease.

If the landlord is not able to secure a release on his assignment of the reversion, then he will be entitled to try again when his successor assigns. The problem, however, is that there is no mechanism proposed for the landlord to receive any notice of that later assignment. The landlord may unwittingly miss his chance. A possible solution would be to include an obligation in the assignment of the reversion for the landlord's successor to notify him in advance of any proposed assignment by that successor of the reversion.

Rent arrears

There are also new rules proposed for arrears of rent and service charge claimed by landlords from previous tenants and/or their guarantors. The old tenant/guarantor has to be notified of such claims by the landlord within nine months of the arrears falling due. It is proposed that this will apply to both existing and future leases.

Avoidance and evasion

The proposed new rules will include anti-avoidance provisions to invalidate any contractual terms that purport to avoid or evade these proposals. The test will be whether the purpose of the relevent contractual term is to avoid these new rules. If so, it will fail the test and will be invalidated.

The solution for landlords might be to look for good commercial reasons why a particular contractual term is needed, so that avoidance of the new rules is an incidental or collateral effect, rather than the purpose of that term. A lease might include an absolute prohibition on assignment, for example, but allow subletting with prior landlords consent. This retains privity of contract between original tenant and landlord, but it would need, in addition, good, commercial reasons to avoid being outlawed by the proposed new rules.

Areas of doubt

The proposed new rules leave a number of areas of doubt. These include:

- Whether the new rules will also apply to residential tenancies.
- Whether the landlord's notice on arrears of rent or service charge is to be served once (so that further accruals would not need to be notified) or whether notification is needed for each payment that becomes due.
- Whether claims for rent and service charge arrears against former tenants are affected by the release of that former tenant's liability on earlier assignment.
- Whether the new rules will try to outlaw all likely terms designed to maintain original tenants' liability or whether, if prevalent, there will be more new rules to outlaw them.
- Whether the guarantee for an incoming tenant can extend beyond the limits of a mere surety, for example, by including indemnity obligations or obliging the guarantor to take up a new lease. This opens up a potential gap between what can be required under the 1988 Act and what can be required under the new legislation.

Impact for landlords

There has been much discussion on the impact for landlords of the release of the original tenant, but the proposed new rules also create a new danger for landlords. This new danger is continuing the original landlord's liability.

Until a release is obtained from the tenant under the procedures set out in the proposed new rules, the original landlord will remain liable for the performance of all the landlord's obligations, notwithstanding an assignment by the landlord of his reversion. This means, for example, where the current landlord failed to reinstate premises destroyed by fire, in breach of a landlord's obligation to do so in the lease, then the tenant could call on the original landlord to rebuild the premises. The impact for such ex-landlords who remain liable, is the risk of substantial contingent liabilities until released.

The position prior to these new rules is that landlords are able to limit their continuing liability by the wording of the lease; and even in poor markets have been able to dictate such terms particularly as it is the landlord's solicitor that usually provides the form of lease. Consequently, landlords have enjoyed a release from liability on sale of their reversions in addition to less onerous covenants in any event.

However, the new rules suggest that all landlords will be tied into their lease obligations for the term of the lease until released by the tenant in accordance with these new rules. The onus would be on the landlord to show whether a release would be reasonable. The new rules outlaw any schemes where the purpose is to avoid these new rules. This means that landlords may not be able to avoid future liability as before. Moreover, the duty to notify tenants of a proposed release of the landlord will delay and complicate the sale of investment property, especially multi-tenanted premises.

Impact on investment

The impact is likely to be in a market where the price for investment property is dictated by the income-yield instead of the growth-yield. This is because the value of such investment depends on cashflow and will consequently be affected by the absence of the guarantee formerly provided by the original tenant's liability.

Two-tier market

Investment property may consequently go through a number of stages. The decline of an investment will apply not only to the premises, but also to the tenant-covenant: this is because each new assignee will signal the end of the prior tenant's liability. The early stages of the lease may appeal to tenants with good covenant-strength, while the later stages of the lease, in a depreciating building, will attract weaker tenants. Landlords potentially faced with this eventuality are advised to consider carefully a refurbishment programme to rejuvenate the cashflow.

The overall effect may be a "two tier" market. The top tier with high rents and limited continuing liability for the tenant under the new rules. The bottom tier with original tenant's liability and lower rents.

CHAPTER 20

Remedy of forfeiture

20.1 Basic rules

The forfeiture clause in a lease is the provision which entitles the landlord to re-enter and take back the premises in certain events. These events will usually be a breach of the terms of the lease by the tenant or non-payment of rent or insolvency.

If the landlord of business premises wants to forfeit the lease then initially it has to decide whether the reason for the forfeiture is non-payment of rent or some other breach of the lease. This is because the procedures and rules that apply to each are different.

If the breach is non-payment of rent then there are some basic rules which need to be followed and these are set out below. If the breach is other than non-payment of rent then in addition to these basic rules there are special procedures under section 146 of the Law of Property Act 1925 that need to be followed and these are also dealt with below.

If the landlord then wants to enforce that right of re-entry possession can be obtained either by taking proceedings to obtain a possession order from the court or by peaceable re-entry. In either case the tenant can claim relief from forfeiture: *Billson* v *Residential Apartments Ltd* [1991] 1 EGLR 70.

The issues which give rise to the basic rules (and which are dealt with further below) are as follows:

- Whether the landlord has a right to forfeit the lease. Such a right is not implied. Moreover, there may be special procedures that need to be followed by the landlord before the right to forfeit arises. These are dealt with further below.

  There are also special procedures which apply where the tenant is in administration, receivership or liquidation and these affect whether the right to forfeit the lease has arisen and if so how it can be enforced.

- Whether the event relied upon is itself sufficient for the right to forfeit to arise. Again such events as the insolvency of the tenant do not automatically enable the landlord to forfeit the lease. It will depend on the terms of the lease. This will need to be checked to ensure that the particular event is covered by the forfeiture clause. However it is common for leases to give the landlord a right to forfeit on the insolvency of the tenant or upon those events which indicate that the tenant is about to become insolvent. Examples are the appointment of an administrator or an arrangement with creditors. Additionally, the lease may provide for forfeiture on bankruptcy of a third party such as the tenant's guarantor or surety.

• Whether the landlord has waived the right to forfeit the lease. This can happen where the landlord has indicated unequivocally that the lease is continuing. This itself will depend upon whether the landlord knew of the breach and whether the breach is a once and for all breach or a continuing breach. This issue is dealt with further below.

• Whether the tenant is seeking relief from forfeiture. The procedures that apply here will depend upon whether the breach is for non-payment of rent or some breach other than non-payment of rent.

Finally this section deals with the type of provisions that should be included in a forfeiture clause to ensure that as few problems as possible are encountered should it be necessary for the landlord to forfeit the lease.

20.2 The right to forfeit

There is no implied right to forfeit the lease although the Law Commission report no 142, 1985 has recommended and advised otherwise. There are two situations in which a lease may be ended despite the absence of a forfeiture clause and these are dealt with below.

It would be rare for a business lease not to include a forfeiture clause, but the first step must always be to check whether the lease contains a forfeiture clause and if so on what events the landlord is entitled to terminate the lease and to take back the premises. The principle here is that if the event on which the landlord is relying meets the forfeiture clause then the lease does not automatically end, but instead there arises a right for the landlord to bring the lease to an end. The lease is not automatically avoided but remains voidable at the option of the landlord: *Jardine* v *Attorney General for Newfoundland* [1932] AC 275. Hence the action taken by the landlord when the right to forfeit has arisen is crucial in determining whether the landlord can enforce that right. If the landlord shows that the lease is to be brought to an end then that right to forfeit the lease has clearly being exercised. Bringing the lease to an end will be evidenced by taking possession proceedings or peaceably re-entering the premises. Equally the landlord is in danger of waiving the right to forfeit by doing something which unequivocably indicates that the lease continues.

Quite separate from the presence or absence of a forfeiture clause it is also possible for the lease to be brought to an end because the tenant has breached a condition which formed the basis of the lease being granted in the first place. This will only arise where the condition either in the lease or agreed after it between the parties makes it clear that the lease will come to an end, if that condition is not fulfilled. This would be a matter of interpretation on the form of words used: *Bashir* v *Commissioner of Lands* [1960] AC 44.

A second example of circumstances in which the landlord may re-enter, even if there is no express right to do so in the lease, is where the tenant acts in a way that denies or prejudices the title of the landlord. It is in the nature of the tenant denying or challenging the landlord's title to the property so as to repudiate the relationship between them as landlord and tenant in the same way that a contract can be repudiated but, as such, it is not an approach that the court may be willing to follow in future: *WG Clark (Properties) Ltd* v *Dupre Properties Ltd* [1991] 2 EGLR 59 and indeed the Law Commission report no 142, 1985 has advised in similar terms.

If there is a right to forfeit under the lease or otherwise then the following matters need to be considered before forfeiture proceedings begin:

A proper demand for rent
It is common for a modern business lease to provide that rent is due whether or not a formal demand has been made. However, where there is no such provision the rent must first be properly demanded before forfeiture proceedings can begin. This means a demand by the landlord, for the rent due at the premises, when the payment is due, both before and until sunset, on that day. This is a rather involved procedure which is why modern leases provide that no formal demand is needed. Otherwise the only exception to this rule is where there is at least half a year's rent in arrears and insufficient items at the premises on which the landlord could

distrain for the arrears: see Landlord and Tenant Act 1730 section 2 and Law of Procedure Act 1852 and section 210.

Prior leave of the court
This issue arises where the tenant is in liquidation. The position depends on whether the liquidation is voluntary or compulsory. If the liquidation is voluntary then the landlord's right to forfeit is not affected, but in exercising the right to forfeit there is a risk to the landlord that an application may be made to the court by the liquidator or any creditor or contributory under section 126 of the Insolvency Act 1986 and in those circumstances the court can exercise the same powers it would have in a compulsory winding up.

Where the tenant is in compulsory liquidation no leave of the court is required to forfeit before the winding-up order is made (but after the petition is presented), but leave of the court is needed when the winding-up order has been made: see section 130(2) of the Insolvency Act 1986.

The tactic for the landlord might be to wait and see how the liquidator proposes to deal with the premises and whether as a result the rent might be claimed as an expense of the liquidation; especially if the liquidator has retained the premises or used it in order to sell the assets. The liquidator's hand may be forced in this by serving a notice to elect whether or not to disclaim the lease. The subject of disclaimer and the tenants in liquidation is dealt with more fully below.

20.3 Section 146 procedure
If the landlord is to forfeit the lease for a breach other than non-payment of rent then the procedure under section 146 Law of Property Act 1925 has to be followed before forfeiture is enforced. This would apply where, for example the tenant had failed to repair the premises, or the tenant was using the premises for a purpose other than permitted by the lease, or had allowed any third party to occupy the premises when there was an absolute prohibition in the lease from doing so.

Before enforcing forfeiture, the landlord has to serve notice on the tenant under section 146 of the Law of Property Act 1925. The notice has to specify the breach and, where it can be remedied require the tenant to do so and to make compensation in money for the breach. The tenant has a reasonable time in which to remedy

the breach and to make monetary
breach. The same section 146 also s.
tenant to obtain relief from forfeiture and ,
below.

It is possible that a breach by the tenant is no.
and in those circumstances the section 146 notic.
to require the tenant to make good that breach. How.
be prudent to provide in the section 146 notice that .
should remedy the breach if that can be done. Certain breac. .re
irremediable such as unlawful assignment or subletting or the
liquidation or bankruptcy of the tenant. An example of a breach
which can be remedied is a failure to repair or an unauthorised use.

In addition, there are special rules which apply under section 146
to the following:

- Agricultural land.
- Mines or minerals.
- A house used or intended to be used as a public house or beer
  shop.
- House let as a dwelling with furniture or other chattels.
- Any property where the personal qualifications of the tenant
  preserve its value or character or are important on the ground of
  neighbourhood to the landlord or person holding under him.

In these situations no notice is required under section 146 where
the tenant is bankrupt or in liquidation. In situations other than
those listed above, if the tenant is bankrupt or in liquidation section
146(10) provides that the notice is required during the first year of
the bankruptcy or the liquidation, but not thereafter: see section
146(9) and (10) and also section 205 of the Law of Property Act
1925.

In all cases it is advisable for the landlord to check that these
matters have been dealt with prior to commencing forfeiture
proceedings.

For further discussion on section 146 notices see also Chapter
11.1.5.

20.4 Landlord's waiver

The initial position, already described, is that when a right to forfeit
the lease has arisen the landlord, in effect, has an option to
determine the lease or to allow it to continue. There is a risk for the
landlord, therefore, that he may have waived his right to forfeit if he

something which unequivocally indicates the lease is continuing despite the breach.

Types of knowledge
This means that the landlord has to know about the breach, in order to waive his right to forfeit. Knowing about the breach, here, means actual or imputed knowledge but not constructive knowledge. Actual knowledge means what the word suggests: that the landlord actually knows that the tenant is in breach of the lease. (An example is shown in *Metropolitan Properties Co Ltd* v *Cordery* (1979) 251 EG 567.) However, the landlord is not bound by constructive knowledge of a breach of the lease by the tenants. An example of constructive knowledge is where the winding up of the tenant has been published through the *London Gazette* but the landlord remains unaware of this and accepts rent in the face of that: *Official Custodian for Charities* v *Parway Estates Developments Ltd* (1984) 270 EG 1077. Imputed knowledge is actual knowledge imputed to the landlord through his agent or representative.

Whether knowledge is actual, imputed or constructive the burden is on the tenant to show that the landlord knew about the breach or had notice of it: *Matthews* v *Smallwood* [1910] 1 Ch 777.

Types of waiver
There is a distinction between waivers which arise from a demand for, or acceptance of rent, and waivers which arise from some other action by the landlord that indicates the lease unequivocally continues. Where rent has been accepted or demanded in the face of a breach by the tenant, this is usually fatal. However, where the action by the landlord is something other than an acceptance or demand for rent then the court will often look at the surrounding circumstances and decide whether, objectively, the landlord's action is so clear as to indicate that the lease is continuing.

Here are some examples of waiver:

- Where the landlord distrains for rent: *Doe'd David* v *Williams* (1835) 7 C&P 322.
- Where the landlord accepts rent for a period after the breaches by the tenant (*Dendy* v *Nicholl* (1858) 4 CBNS 376) although accepting rent for the period prior to the breach is not a waiver: *Price* v *Worwood* (1859) 4 H&N 512.
- Where the landlord accepts rent without prejudice to the right to

forfeit: *Segal Securities Ltd* v *Thoseby* [1963] 1 QB 887. Although there is no waiver where the landlord enters into negotiations with the tenant without prejudice to his right to forfeit: *Re National Jazz Centre Ltd* [1988] 2 EGLR 57. It is also relevant whether the landlord actually demands the rent or simply receives it from the tenant and whether the landlord returns it if received in ignorance of the breach: see *John Lewis Properties plc* v *Viscount Chelsea* [1993] 34 EG 116.

There is also a distinction made between the one-off breach and a continuing breach. The difference is relevant to the landlord in that a continuing breach is a breach which reoccurs each day, such that waiver by the landlord may not be fatal.

This is because waiver only operates to past breaches: *Penton* v *Barnett* [1898] 1 QB 276. Where the breach is a continuing breach the right for the landlord to forfeit the lease similarly continues and a waiver by the landlord at any point will not prevent the landlord from exercising the right to forfeit the lease if at the point of forfeiture the breach was continuing.

Here are some examples of one-off breaches:

- Non-payment of rent or other sums reserved as rent under the lease such as the insurance, service charge or VAT.
- The making of an administration order or the appointment of a receiver or liquidator: although in each case the terms of the forfeiture clause will need to be checked to ensure that it fits the particular circumstances.
- Alterations carried out where there is an absolute prohibition on such in the lease.
- An assignment or subletting or sharing of possession with the premises again where the lease prohibits such.

Where the landlord has waived the right to forfeit he is still entitled to proceed with the other remedies (see below). However, it is unlikely that the usual clause often found in a commercial lease concerning waivers is effective: such a clause normally provides that demand for or the acceptance of rent by the landlord or its agents in the face of a breach does not constitute a waiver. It is suggested that the court will take the same approach to such clauses as it does to the acceptance of rent by the landlord without prejudice to his right to forfeit the lease: see above and also see *R* v *Paulson* [1921] 1 AC 271.

20.5 The tenant's relief

Where the landlord has a right to forfeit the lease, the law does allow the tenant an opportunity to make good the breach, whether the breach is for non-payment of rent or otherwise; and in either case the court has power to exercise its discretion to give the tenant another chance. This is reflected in the procedure that the landlord needs to follow before enforcing his right to forfeiture and the different remedies available to the tenant in seeking relief, depending on whether the breach is one of non-payment of rent, or some other covenant in the lease. It also depends on whether the forfeiture was enforced peaceably or by proceedings.

Non-payment of rent: peaceable re-entry

In the county court the rules of equity apply and there are no statutory time-limits. Equity which originated the power to grant relief in forfeiture cases, regarded the power to forfeit for non payment of rent as a mere security: *Howard* v *Fanshawe* [1895] 2 Ch 581. The court will usually grant relief at any time up to six months from the date of peaceable re-entry.

In the High Court the rules of equity also apply, but again six months is likely to be the usual period during which relief will be granted. Again the court has direction to grant relief at any time and on such terms as it thinks fit.

Non-payment of rent: court proceedings

In the county court sections 138 and 139 of the County Courts Act 1984 apply. There is automatic relief if the tenant pays all arrears and costs of the action into court not less than five clear days before the return day. Alternatively, the court can make an order for possession suspended for not less than four weeks. If the tenant pays the arrears and costs within the that period of suspension the lease is reinstated. However, costs will not necessarily be on an indemnity basis: *Billson* v *Residential Apartments Ltd.*

Otherwise, the tenant must apply for a relief within six months of the enforcement of the order for possession. Section 138 (9A) (inserted by section 55 Administration of Justice Act 1985) the court will grant relief on such terms as it thinks fit.

In the High Court there is relief under section 38 of the Supreme Court Act 1981. The tenants application must be made within six months of execution of the judgement of possession. If all arrears and costs are paid relief will normally be granted.

Relief against forfeiture for other breaches
In these cases a section 146 notice must be served. The court has discretion as to whether relief should be granted. A tenant cannot apply for relief after a landlord has forfeited a lease by proceedings and entered into possession.

However, a tenant can apply for relief after a landlord has forfeited by peaceable re-entry. The period during which it can apply for relief after a landlord has forfeited by peaceable re-entry is uncertain. Lord Templeman in *Billson* v *Residential Apartments Ltd* indicated "a reasonable time".

Mortgagees and subtenants
If the tenant's lease is forfeited, any subtenancy also falls away. However, section 146(4) Law of Property Act 1925 enables a subtenant to apply for an entirely new lease subject to appropriate conditions. Both mortgagees and subtenants can apply for relief within six months (or even later) of the landlord taking possession under section 38 of the Supreme Court Act 1981 and section 138 of the County Courts Act 1984. This is shown in *Eaton Square Properties Ltd* v *Burridge* [1993] EGCS 91 and also in *United Dominions Trust Ltd* v *Shellpoint Trustees Ltd* [1993] EGCS 57. The former case deals with subtenants and the latter with mortgagees.

20.6 Forfeiture clause

Since there is no implied right for the landlord to forfeit (subject to the two exceptions dealt with above), it is imperative that the forfeiture clause in the lease adequately covers all the likely events that the landlord will want to rely on: in taking back the premises in the event of a breach by the tenant of its terms, or if tenant becomes insolvent. At the very least, the landlord should be entitled to take back the premises if the rent is, in whole or in part unpaid after becoming due. This should be whether the rent is formally demanded or not, as this would avoid the need for the landlord to follow the archaic procedure involved in demanding rent: see earlier.

In drafting terms the forfeiture clause should cover all the rents reserved under the lease, which means that not only the rent but also the insurance premium, service charge and VAT should be reserved as rent. This preserves the landlord's rights for distress as well as for forfeiture (although the landlord cannot pursue both remedies at the same time). The forfeiture clause also needs to extend, at the very least, to any breach or non-performance or non-observance by the tenant of any of the terms of the lease.

Additionally, where the tenant is a limited company the following insolvency events should be included:

- Where the tenant enters into liquidation whether compulsory or voluntary (unless it is for reconstruction or amalgamation of a solvent company).
- Where the tenant passes a resolution for winding up (unless it is, as before, for reconstruction or amalgamation of a solvent company).
- Where the tenant is deemed unable to pay its debts as defined in section 123 of the Insolvency Act 1986.
- Where the tenant has a receiver manager or administrative receiver or provisional liquidator or administrator appointed.
- Where the tenant makes a proposal for a voluntary arrangement under Part I of the Insolvency Act 1986 or for a similar arrangement under section 425 of the Companies Act 1985.
- Where the tenant has a petition for an administration order made in relation to it.

Where the tenant is an individual then the following events should trigger forfeiture:

- Where there is the presentation of a bankruptcy petition or circumstances where such petition may be presented under Part IX of the Insolvency Act 1986.
- Where a voluntary arrangement or an interim order under the Insolvency Act 1986 is made or applied for.
- Where a receiver is appointed under the Mental Health Act 1983.

Similarly these events might be extended from the tenant to any guarantor for the tenant under the lease. It should also extend to circumstances where either the tenant or the guarantor enter into an arrangements or compositions with its creditors or suffer distress or execution on its goods.

The forfeiture clause, then, needs to make it clear that in all such circumstances the landlord, is then entitled to re-enter the premises, or any part of it, upon which the lease ends. However, such automatic termination of the lease will need to be stated to be without prejudice to any right or remedy of the landlord for any antecedent breach, non-observance or non-performance of the terms of the lease by the tenant.

CHAPTER 21

Remedy of distress

Distress is a remedy which allows a bailiff instructed by the landlord (or the landlord in person) to seize goods on the premises whether belonging to the tenant or other people.

The Law Commission report no 194, 1991 – has recommended the abolition of this remedy as it gives landlords priority over other creditors and prejudices third parties (if any) whose goods are distrained. However, when there is no administration, liquidation or bankruptcy (when different rules apply and are dealt with elsewhere below) distress remains a valuable remedy for non-payment of rent. Before levying distress the landlord must consider whether the value of the remedy in each particular case lies in its threat or its execution. If it is intended to execute and complete the distress, then there must be goods at the premises worth seizing and selling, otherwise the remedy has no value.

21.1 When and for what
When may distress be levied
There must be an existing relationship of landlord and tenant and the distress must only be to recover rent. However, a written lease is not required and an agreement for lease can be sufficient to allow distress to be exercised. Distress may not be levied if there is only a licence as there is no relationship of landlord and tenant, eg there may not be distress during any holding over unless it is a statutory continuation.

The exception is under section 6 Landlord and Tenant Act 1709 where a lease has expired and, provided the former tenant remains in occupation a landlord can distrain for rent accrued up to the expiry of the lease for six months after the expiry of the tenancy.

For what may distress be levied
Distress may be levied for rent only. However, it is not clear whether service charge or insurance premiums are "rent" for these purposes (even if reserved as rent in the lease). This is because, it is argued,

service charges and for example, are often subject to tests of reasonableness, and as such may be queried under the lease by the tenant and are therefore, arguably, uncertain.

21.2 Who and what
Who can levy distress
The following can levy distress:

- The landlord for the relevant period while it is landlord. If the landlord's interest is sold the new landlord cannot distrain for arrears accrued prior to the sale.
- A mortgagee may distrain on the tenant of the mortgagor after serving notice of its intention to take possession or receive rents.
- The personal representatives may distrain if the deceased landlord could have distrained under section 26(4) of the Administration of Estates Act 1925.
- A receiver appointed by the court or a mortgagee can distrain under section 101(1)(iii) of the Law of Property Act 1925.

In practice the landlord, or a certified bailiff will levy distress, but the landlord will be liable for any wrongful acts of his bailiff. In terms of the bailiff's fees only scale costs are recoverable under the Distress for Rent Rules 1988 whatever else the lease may provide.

What can be seized
The landlord or the bailiff can seize anything which can be removed without damage to the premises unless excluded or privileged at law. These exclusions or privileged items include the following:

- Goods in actual use.
- Goods already taken by the sheriff in execution.
- Goods given for the purposes of a public trade, eg a watch left to be mended.
- Tenant's fixtures.

There is also some protection for the goods of an undertenant paying full value for the underlet premises and the goods of a lodger or a mortgagee or other third party: see the Law of Distress Amendment Act 1908.

Distress may not be levied on a Sunday and only after sunrise or before sunset, and after the date the rent becomes due, ie not on the quarter day and only during the term of the tenancy unless section 6 of the Landlord and Tenant Act 1709 applies (see above).

The maximum amount which can be recovered by distress is six-years' rent.

Distress can only be levied on the premises for which the rent is payable. Entry cannot be obtained by breaking in by force therefore, eg only open windows may be used.

21.3 The sale
The procedure
Notice of the distress and memorandum thereof is delivered to the tenant or left on the premises setting out the amount being distrained for, bailiff's fees, charges and expenses. The tenant must also be given the scale of charges. The goods seized are then treated as "impounded". Such goods may removed from the premises or (more likely) the tenant will enter into a "walking possession" agreement not to remove them. The goods can then remain and be used by the tenant, but not removed from the premises. Five-clear days must then elapse before the goods can be sold. The tenant can request an extension to 15 days. The landlord can still sue for any shortfall after the sale. The sale need not be by auction, but the landlord must get the best price and this can create problems of proof. Any residue after the sale and payment of arrears and expenses is payable to the tenant.

The right to distrain ends when the relationship of landlord and tenant ends; or when landlord has a judgment for the outstanding rent or on the unconditional tender of the rent due to the landlord. In such case the landlord must return the goods distrained.

Should the landlord levy distress
These are the issues to consider before levying distress.
- The likely value of the goods that may be distrained.
- The likely proportion of third-party goods at the premises; there are likely to be more goods on hire in office premises as opposed to industrial or retail premises where there may be valuable stock.
- The likely negotiating position of the respective parties: this is relevant where the liquidator, trustee or receiver of the tenant is simply withholding rent prior to a sale of valuable assets of the business at the premises.

If the tenant illegally repossesses goods that is "pound breach" and the landlord may treble the rent. If the landlord unlawfully distrains the tenant can recover double damages. A tenant who fraudulently or clandestinely removes goods to avoid distress risks seizure of double their value by the landlord within 30 days of the goods removal (Distress for Rent Act 1737), although the landlord has to find the goods and prove the removal was fraudulent.

CHAPTER 22

Tenant in administration

Administration is a process under the Insolvency Act 1986 which enables a company to be placed into a protective period during which the business can be saved and possibly rescued from liquidation or receivership. The need for such a procedure came out of the *Cork Report*. It was noted that receivers appointed pursuant to a debenture containing a floating charge might be able to rescue a company, but that such a procedure was not available where there was no floating charge enabling a receiver to be appointed. Consequently, the Insolvency Act 1986 created a procedure for the court to appoint an administrator, akin to a receiver, to achieve such purposes which are set out in a court order.

This procedure enables a rescue operation to be put together in those situations where a receiver or manager could not otherwise be appointed because there is no creditor with a floating charge over the assets of the business.

The idea is to encourage early action. A board of directors in severe financial difficulties might consider it prudent to seek outside help quickly and to hand over control of the company to a professional person to act as administrator, rather than let a potentially insolvent situation worsen. The objective, perhaps, for the directors being to reduce the risk of personal liability under section 214 of the Insolvency Act 1986 for wrongful trading since the appointment of an administrator would help the directors to show that every prudent, practical step had been taken to reduce potential loss to creditors from an insolvent liquidation.

Whatever the reasons for the appointment of the administrator there are a number of consequences which the landlord will need to consider when faced with a tenant in administration.

22.1 How administration works
The petition
The appointment of an administrator results from a petition to the court presented either by the company, its directors or a creditor.

A clerk of the magistrates court (under section 87 Magistrates Court Act 1980) may also present a petition in relation to an outstanding fine.

Where the landlord has outstanding rent arrears it has status as a creditor to apply to the court for an administration order. However, the effect of the administration order is to restrict the remedies available to the landlord. Consequently the landlord may be better off considering alternative remedies against the original tenant, intermediate tenants, guarantors or in forcing liquidation of the tenant. Nevertheless, the landlord will need to be aware of his position following the administration order, if made, because of its impact on the usual remedies otherwise available against the tenant.

The order and its effect
If the court is satisfied that the company is unable to pay its debts and considers that the purposes of the administration order will be likely to be achieved, then the court will make an administration order under section 8 of the Insolvency Act 1986. For these purposes the inability to pay debts is more fully defined in section 123 of the Insolvency Act 1986, but includes, among other things, where the tenant company in unable to pay its debts as they fall due or where the value of its assets is less than the amount of its liabilities taking into account its contingent and prospective liabilities.

The purposes for which the administration order may be made are as follows:

- The survival of the company and its undertaking as a going concern.
- The approval of a voluntary arrangement under Part I of the Insolvency Act 1986.
- The sanctioning of a compromise or arrangement between the company and its creditors under section 425 of the Companies Act 1985 and
- A more advantageous realisation of the company's assets than would be effected on a winding up.

Where there is already an administrative receiver in place the order may not be made without his consent; unless the court is shown that the debenture or floating charge by which the receiver was appointed is, in fact, void or likely to be set aside as a preference or as a transaction at an undervalue. The court is also likely to have regard to the report filed by the proposed administrator, who has to be a licenced insolvency practitioner, and which will set out whether any of the purposes for which an order may be made are likely to be achieved.

The petition has to be served on, among others, anyone who has been appointed an administrative receiver or who is entitled to make such an appointment and on anyone who has presented a winding-up petition against the company. The full list of those on whom the petition has to be served is set out in rule 2.6 of the Insolvency Rules 1986. However a landlord is not among those listed in those rules and since the presentation of the petition is not listed in the *London Gazette* or anywhere else, a landlord may simply be unaware that a petition has been presented until after the order has been made.

However, the restrictions on a landlord's remedies operate immediately from the presentation of the petition. From the date the petition is presented and until the administration order is made (or the petition is dismissed) the following apply:

- No steps can be taken to enforce any security over the company's assets, including its property, or to repossess goods in the company's possession under any hire-purchase agreements, without the leave of the court. This prevents the landlord from exercising the remedy of forfeiture by peaceable re-entry: *Exchange Travel Agency Ltd* v *Triton Property Trust plc* [1991] 2 EGLR 50.
- No steps may be taken to bring other proceedings nor any execution or other legal process against the company or its property without the court's leave. This means that the landlord's remedy of distress will not be available during this period.

When the administration order has been made the following restrictions apply:

- No petition for the winding up of the company can be presented; any existing petition is dismissed; any administrative receiver has to vacate office; no further receiver may be appointed.
- No other steps may be taken to enforce any security over the company's property and no other proceedings or execution or other legal process may be started without the consent of the administrator or the leave of the court.

The full detail of the limitations arising on the administration order are set out in section 11 of the Insolvency Act 1986. For the landlord it means that the remedy of distress and the remedy of forfeiture are both limited by the consent of the administrator or the leave of the court.

22.2 The administrator's position
Powers
The administrator is in a very similar position to that of the administrative receiver and in the same way acts as agent of the company under section 14 of the Insolvency Act 1986. For the landlord this means that he can deal with the administrator who will be acting on behalf of the tenant, but, as agent, he will not be personally liable on any contracts made on behalf of that company while he makes clear that he acts as agent only. The contrast is with the administrative receiver who is personally liable on contracts unless there is an express exclusion of personal liability in the contract: section 37 Insolvency Act 1986.

The powers of the administrator under section 14 of the Insolvency Act 1986 are those set out in Schedule 1 to that Act. They include the following:

- The power to manage and to deal with the company's property.
- The power to borrow money and grant security.
- The power to take possession of and collect the property of the company.
- The power to grant or accept a surrender of a lease or tenancy of any property of the company or take a lease or tenancy which is required or convenient for the company's business.
- The power to carry on the business of the company.

Generally the administrator has power to do all things that are necessary for the management of the affairs of the business and property of the company; although a landlord dealing with the administrator in good faith does not have to check that the administrator is acting within his powers. The landlord has the protection given to any other third party dealing with the administration under section 14 of the Insolvency Act 1986.

The administrator also has power to dispose of any property which is subject to a floating charge as if it were not subject to that floating charge. However the administrator may not dispose of property subject to a fixed charge unless:

- The mortgagor consents (and would therefore provide a release for the property from the fixed charge or mortgage).
- The administrator obtains the court's leave, which will only be given if it is shown that the sale of the assets freed from the fixed charge would be likely to promote the purposes specified in the administration order.

Where the property is subject to a charge then the administrator's power to grant leases is limited to restrictions further described in section 15 of the Insolvency Act 1986.

Duties
The administrator is obliged to take control of the company and its assets which would include any leasehold premises and tenant's fixtures and fittings at those premises. The administrator has three months in which to make a proposal to a creditors meeting for achieving the purpose or purposes set out in the administration order. Before those proposals are approved, the administrator has to act as the court directs; but, once approved, the administrator acts in accordance with the terms of that proposal. There are also rules pursuant to section 21 of the Insolvency Act 1986 for the administrator to notify creditors, Companies Registry and the *London Gazette* of the administration order.

If the administrator's proposals are rejected by the creditors meeting then the court has a number of alternative options as follows:

- To discharge the administration order.
- To adjourn matters generally.
- To make an interim order.
- To make any other order that it thinks fit.

22.3 The landlord's position
Restrictions on remedies
The combined effect of the presentation of a petition and of the administration order is that the following remedies are not available to a landlord except either with the leave of the court or the consent of the administrator: see sections 10 and 11 of the Insolvency Act 1986:

- The remedy of forfeiture.
- The remedy of distress.
- The remedy of action against the tenant in administration.

Where the consent of the administrator is not forthcoming (or not applicable in the case of the period following the presentation of the petition and before the order) then the landlord will be left with an application to court for leave to commence proceedings. The court has power to make such order as it thinks fit, but will probably take account of the nature and extent of the breaches of covenant (in particular the amount of rent arrears and the state of the premises) and also the likelihood of the lease being acquired by the administrator either to continue the business or to dispose of it as a going concern.

Guidelines for the court in granting leave under section 11 of the Insolvency Act 1986 were given in *Re Atlantic Computer Systems plc* [1990] 1 All ER 476. Although the case was not directly concerned with the position of a landlord the relevant principles applied to a landlord's situation results as follows:

- Where the landlord is seeking leave to commence proceedings the onus will be on the landlord to make out a case.
- Where the landlord is seeking to forfeit the lease and recover possession, the court will weigh up the conflicting interests of the landlord against those of the tenant's other creditors.
- Where the court is weighing up these conflicting interests it will attach greater importance to the proprietary interest of the landlord against that of the unsecured creditors.

The presentation of the petition and/or the order does not affect any of the following landlords remedies:

- The remedy against an original tenant (if this is not the tenant in administration).
- The right of action against intermediate tenants prior to the immediate tenant, where those intermediate tenants have contracted with the landlord to make good any breach of the lease or rent arrears.
- The remedy against guarantors of intermediate or original tenants (depending on the terms of the guarantee).

The landlord's options
Where the landlord is aware that an administration petition has been presented and the order has not yet been made, then the landlord may consider whether he should, individually, or with others present a petition for the liquidation of the company. This does not require the leave of the court under section 10 of the

Insolvency Act 1986 and would then entitle the landlord to appear before the court when it considers making an administration order. The landlord will have an interest in the making of that order under section 11 of the Insolvency Act 1986 and his petition will be dismissed if the order is made; but this gives the landlord an opportunity to present his case to the court before it makes the administration order.

If the landlord wants to prevent the administration order being made so as to preserve its usual remedies as landlord, then the options are as follows:

- to persuade a debenture holder, if any, which has the benefit of a floating charge to appoint an administrative receiver before the administration order is made. This is because the court will not appoint an administrator where there is a receiver appointed unless the appointment of the receiver is defective or the appointor of the receiver consents: see section 9 of the Insolvency Act 1986. However, this option will only be of use to the landlord if, as part of the appointment of the receiver, a deal is struck between the appointor and the landlord on the payment of the rent arrears as part of the administrative receivership.
- to persuade the court, either that the company is able to pay its debts, or that the administration order would be unlikely to achieve the purposes set out in section 8 of the Insolvency Act 1986. This option is unlikely to be of much use to the landlord unless it has detailed knowledge of the company and its affairs. However other creditors and may have useful information to assist on this.

Generally the landlord should also look at the other options normally available and not affected by the administration order. These include action against the original tenant, intermediate tenants and/or guarantors.

Collecting rent
While the tenant is in administration it remains liable for the rent even though the administrator is now running it. However it is not certain that the rent will be paid and action against the tenant in administration cannot be taken to recover the rent without the consent of the administrator or the leave of the court. Nevertheless, the administrator is an officer of the court and as such, has to act responsibly in paying debts as they fall due; and if the administrator

does not do so, the landlord should consider whether an application can be made to the court for leave to take action against the tenant in administration for the rent arrears.

If rent is not paid, then the landlord still has the remedy of forfeiture or distress, but the leave, of the court will be needed. If the court refuses leave, it may still order the administrator to pay rent as it becomes due, particularly if the administrator can be shown to have acted unreasonably in not paying the rent during the administration. The administrator is not personally liable for the rent or the terms of the lease unless he enters into a new contract which makes him so liable.

Dealings

Where a petition for an administration order has been made against the tenant, it is unsafe for the landlord to enter into any further dealings with that tenant, but instead the landlord should look at the options available following presentation of a petition and before the order is made.

If the administration order is made then all subsequent dealings must be with the administrator, who is then empowered by the order to act as agent for the company with all the usual powers set out in Schedule 1 to the Insolvency Act 1986. This is particularly relevant where the landlord is negotiating a deal with the director/guarantors or following the administration order is taking action against original or intermediate tenants. Any proposal to reassign or surrender the lease by a tenant in administration has to be executed by the administrator.

CHAPTER 23

Tenant in receivership

23.1 What how and when of receiverships
Types of receiverships

Where a business tenant has borrowed money it will usually be required to provide security for those borrowings and this might comprise the lease and the company's other assets. The receivership is a mechanism by which the lender can realise its security regardless of the interests of the other creditors or of the tenant company.

Security

There are a variety of receivers and receiverships for both individuals and limited companies, but the most common and relevant to the tenant in receivership are as follows:

- The receiver appointed under a fixed charge or mortgage by section 109 of the Law of Property Act 1925. This is known as an LPA receiver.
- The receiver appointed under a floating charge over the whole or substantially the whole of the company's property and regulated by the Insolvency Act 1986. In a debenture it would not be unusual for the lease to form part of the fixed charge and for the debenture to include a floating charge over the assets of the tenant company. Such an arrangement also falls within the definition of section 29 of the Insolvency Act 1986 and such a receiver is known as the administrative receiver.
- There are also provisions in the Insolvency Act 1986 for the appointment of a receiver by the court.

The appointment of a LPA receiver is only likely to be relevant where the lease has a capital value in the open market. This arises where there is a long lease at a ground rent. A normal commercial lease of, for example, 25 years at a rack-rent with five-year reviews will not usually have such a capital value and will more likely form part of the assets of the company secured generally under a debenture containing both fixed and floating charges.

The provisions applying to LPA receivers are dealt with in section 23.3 and otherwise this remaining section deals with the position on the appointment of an administrative receiver over the assets of a business tenant company.

Procedure

The administrative receiver can be appointed by the court but most are appointed by the holders of a debenture. The administrative receiver appointed by the court is an officer of that court and is not the company's agent. His powers and duties will be controlled by the terms of the court order.

The administrative receiver appointed by a debenture holder will act as the company agent under section 44 of the Insolvency Act 1986 and his powers and duties would be determined by the terms of the debenture and supplemented/regulated by the Insolvency Act 1986. Although the administrative receiver is appointed by the lender he is the agent of the company tenant because he is paid by that tenant in realising the tenant's assets to pay off the debt to the lender. The administrative receiver is appointed when there has been some breach of the terms of the debenture, mortgage or floating charge and the debenture holder then decides to appoint a receiver.

The administrative receiver has to be a licensed insolvency practitioner (see section 230 of the Insolvency Act 1986) and for the appointment to be valid, it has to be accepted before the end of the next business day after receipt by the receiver of the appointment: see section 33 of the Insolvency Act 1986. The Insolvency Rules 1986 also provide that the appointment has to be accepted in writing within seven days of the appointment. The lender appointing the receiver must also within seven days of the appointment notify the registrar of companies under section 405 of the Companies Act 1985. The appointment is also advertised in the *London Gazette* and all the usual paperwork for the tenants business, including invoices letters and orders have to contain a statement that a receiver or manager has been appointed.

Debentures often provide that before an administrative receiver can be appointed the lender has to serve a demand on the tenant company for payment of all money due. If the lender seeks to appoint an administrative receiver for any other default of the terms of the debenture then it will need to show that such an event has occurred. The demand for all money due need not specify an exact amount, but it is good practice to do so.

More than one administrative receiver can be appointed. It is common for at least two receivers to be appointed jointly and severally. The landlord should therefore check the terms of the appointment and of the debenture to ensure that he is dealing with the right person, who is authorised to do what he is claiming to do.

Agent of the tenant

The administrative receiver is appointed by the lender, but will act as agent of the business tenant. The tenant will always be a company and not an individual for an administrative receiver to be appointed as an individual cannot create a floating charge. An administrative receiver is a receiver or manager of the whole or substantially the whole of the company's property appointed by or on behalf of the holders of a debenture of the company secured by a charge which as such was a floating charge or included a floating charge: see section 29 of the Insolvency Act 1986.

The terms of the floating charge or debenture will normally expressly state that the receiver will act as agent for the tenant, but otherwise section 44 of the Insolvency Act 1986 provides that the receiver will be deemed the company's agent until the company goes into liquidation.

An administrative receiver is personally liable on any contract he enters into unless the contract otherwise provides. It is therefore common, if not invariably the case, that all contracts entered into by receivers will contain specific provisions excluding the personal liability of the receiver. The risk for the receiver if the tenant is already in liquidation, is that he may become liable personally on contracts entered into by him; although he will still be able to exclude his personal liability, if a liquidator has authorised the receiver to continue to act as agent for the tenant company. Again the key point remains that it is vital for the landlord in all dealings with the tenant in receivership to identify with whom he is dealing and the status of the tenant company at the time when any contract or dealing is entered into.

The other point that the landlord needs to remember is that the administrative receiver is only the manager and receiver of the company's property. The tenant as an original party to any contract, in particular the lease, remains liable upon its terms and the receiver has no power to release the tenant company from the terms of the lease and no power to disclaim the lease (such a power to disclaim is only available to a liquidator or trustee in bankruptcy which is dealt with in more detail below).

The receiver can opt to take no action at all, including non-payment of rent without being liable, as the receiver is not liable for contracts entered into prior to the receivership. However in those circumstances all the usual remedies still remain available to the landlord to enforce the terms of the lease. The only remedy which loses its value is that of suing the tenant itself: the appointment of the receiver, if nothing else, indicates that the tenant company is probably not worth pursuing, particularly where the lender's security under its debenture exceeds the value of the company's assets. However, the remaining remedies of suing the original tenant, intermediate tenant, guarantors and the alternative remedies of forfeiture or distress still remain available. Indeed the appointment of a receiver may itself be an event giving rise to the right for the landlord to forfeit the lease.

23.2 The administrative receiver's position
Powers

The administrative receiver has a number of powers contained in part in the debenture or charge under which it is appointed and in part by the Insolvency Act 1986, Schedule 1. The powers set out in Schedule 1 to the Insolvency Act 1986 include the following:

- The power to take possession of the property.
- The power to sell or dispose of property.
- The power to make any payment necessary to the performance of the receiver's functions.
- The power to carry on the business of the company.

This means that the landlord is able to deal with the receiver as if he were dealing with the directors of the tenant company as the directors have largely been replaced by the receiver who will not be able to interfere with the receiver's function. Indeed the landlord need not enquire as to whether the receiver is acting within his powers because section 42 of the Insolvency Act 1986 effectively provides that if the landlord is acting in good faith and for value he will be protected as far as the receiver's powers are concerned.

Duties

The administrative receiver's main duty will be to realise the property and assets of the business over which he has been appointed by the debenture holder or lender. However the administrative receiver, as agent for the company, also has a subsidiary duty to the tenant and this duty will extend to any guarantor of the tenant's obligations under the mortgage or debenture (*American Express International Banking Corporation* v *Hurley* [1985] 3 All ER 564) and arguably to other chargees of the property: *Midland Bank Ltd* v *Joliman Finance Ltd* (1967) 203 EG 1039. The result is that the administrative receiver has to use reasonable care in exercising its powers to ensure that a proper market value of the assets is realised when the sale is made.

However the administrative receiver has no duty to the landlord to pay the rent, which would otherwise rank along with the other unsecured creditors, but as the landlord retains his right to forfeit the lease or levy distress on the company's assets at the premises, the receiver will need to have regard to the landlord's rent arrears so as to prevent forfeiture or distress.

23.3 The landlord's position
Options available for the landlord
A useful approach for the landlord to take is to consider how the receiver will deal with the problem. The receiver (often appointed by a bank) will want to try if possible to sell the business over which he is appointed receiver as a going concern and, if not, then to realise the best value he can for the assets of the company. Unlike a liquidator, a receiver has no power to disclaim a lease (see below) and so his options are often limited, thus giving a landlord a better scope for negotiation than is usually appreciated by most landlords.

This means that the landlord still retains the following options where a business tenant is in administrative receivership:

- To forfeit the lease.
- To levy distress against any assets at the premises.
- To serve notice on the subtenants, if any, under the Law of Distress Amendment Act 1908 to collect the rent from that subtenant directly.
- To sue for unpaid rent any guarantors of the tenant in administrative receivership.
- To sue for unpaid rent the original tenant and/or its guarantors where the tenant in administrative receivership is an assignee.
- To sue for unpaid rent any intermediate tenants between the original tenant and the tenant in administrative receivership where

such intermediate tenants have entered into a contract by licence to assign to pay rent for the remainder of the term of the lease (and/or sue any guarantors of such intermediate tenants).

The remedy of forfeiture will only be available if the terms of the forfeiture clause in the lease permit it. The key point for the landlord to consider is whether in commercial terms it has an alternative use for the premises and whether it is likely to find a replacement tenant in the current market. Forfeiture of the lease will also stop original and intermediate tenants being liable for unpaid rent up to the date of the forfeiture.

Distress as an alternative remedy for the landlord is more fully dealt with elsewhere. However, the key point for the landlord to consider at this stage is whether there are any assets at the premises against which it is worth levying distress.

Where the tenant is in administrative receivership the choice of remedy will depend on the receiver's position and the options available to him.

Options available for the receiver
If he wishes to retain the lease then, to prevent forfeiture or distress, he must pay the rent (including arrears of rent) and perform the covenants. He will make it clear to the landlord that in doing this he is merely acting on behalf of the tenant and not in any sense in a personal capacity.

If the receiver has no use for the lease (given he has no statutory power to disclaim the lease) he may consider:

• Allowing forfeiture to take place.
• Negotiating a surrender of the lease.
• Persuading the debenture holder to release the lease from the charge.

The landlord should therefore consider which of these options the receiver is likely to exercise and act accordingly. In particular, if the receiver is intending to sell the assets shortly, perhaps as part of the sale of the business as a going concern, the levying of distress on those assets may produce, at least, part payment of the rent arrears, if not all of it.

Similarly, if the receiver has no use for the premises and wants the landlord to forfeit, the landlord should consider the consequential effect on the liability of any original tenant, intermediate tenants or guarantors.

Equally, if there are subtenants of whole or part of the premises, a surrender, rather than forfeiture, would make those subtenants a direct tenant of the landlord and in a poor market that may be of value to the landlord. The subtenant, on the other hand, may prefer the receiver to allow forfeiture to take place, which will leave the subtenant with the option of applying for relief or walking away from the sublease, since forfeiture of an intermediate lease would normally bring the sublease to an end.

23.4 LPA receiver
Generally
An LPA receivership is a particular type of receivership arising under a fixed charge (as opposed to a floating charge), in which the receiver is appointed by a lender who has a legal charge over the property. In the case of an LPA receiver of a business tenant, this will only arise where the lease has been charged by way of legal mortgage and the lender has decided to appoint an LPA receiver to realise the lease. Commercial leases of about 25 years with the usual five-year reviews as to rack-rent will not have much market value making it worthwhile appointing an LPA receiver. Such rack-rent leases can have a premium value in good markets. However, the more likely form of lease having a capital value, will be the long lease or ground lease at a nominal ground rent. A tenant under such a lease may charge it to its lender by way of legal mortgage and on default by the borrower tenant the lender will have power to appoint an LPA receiver.

The value and relevance of an LPA receiver to a lender will usually depend on whether the property needs to be managed and whether there are sublease rents which need to be collected. There is no requirement for the LPA receiver to be a licensed insolvency practitioner. There are arguments for (see *Meadrealm Ltd* v *Transcontinental Golf Construction Ltd* 1992 unreported) and dangers for surveyors or other professionals appointed as LPA receivers where the charge under which the appointment is made includes a floating charge. The only safe position for anyone appointed as LPA receiver, who is not a licensed insolvency practitioner, is to ensure that the appointment arises out of a fixed charge and does not include any assets caused by a floating charge, or to obtain a full indemnity from the appointing lender.

The appointment has to be accepted before the end of the following business day, although this does not have to be in writing.

The power for the lender to appoint the LPA receiver will only arise when that lender is able to exercise its power of sale under the mortgage. This means that the legal charge has to be by deed and the provisions of section 103 of the Law of Property Act 1925 have to be complied with (although these provisions are usually amended under the terms of the legal charge itself).

The LPA receiver's position

The powers of the LPA receiver are limited to those set out in section 109 of the Law of Property Act 1925, but supplemented by any additional powers included in the legal charge itself. The powers under section 109 of the Law of Property Act include the following:

- The power to recover all income (which will include rent) from the property over which the receiver is appointed by action or by levying distress or otherwise.
- To keep back from any money received sufficient for the receiver's own fees and expenses incurred by him as receiver.
- The power to insure the property if directed to do so by the lender.

There is no power for the LPA receiver to sell the property in the Law of Property Act 1925. This means that the legal charge must contain and extend those powers to enable the LPA receiver to deal with the property and to manage the tenants business. However, the LPA receiver has no power to disclaim a lease, such power is only available to a liquidator or a trustee in bankruptcy.

There are also limited powers for the LPA receiver to lease property under section 99 of the Law of Property Act 1925. Again these are usually modified by the terms of the legal charge itself.

The landlord's position

The LPA receiver has no power to disclaim the lease, but is not personally liable on contracts entered into prior to his appointment, which will include the lease. Any contract entered into by the LPA receiver after his appointment will usually make it clear that the LPA receiver is acting as agent for the tenant and is not personally liable under such contract.

The landlord therefore has largely the same options available to him as he has against the administrative receiver. There may be little value in pursuing the tenant in receivership especially since the

LPA receiver is not personally liable on the rent unless he agrees to assume personal liability. However, the landlord will still have the option of pursuing any original tenant, intermediate tenant or guarantors. There will also be the alternative remedies of forfeiture and distress.

CHAPTER 24

Tenant in liquidation

The position here is different from a company tenant in receivership. The liquidator is involved in a process of winding up the company and so has a different approach. It is therefore important for the landlord to appreciate the options available to the liquidator so as to know how best to negotiate with him. An important issue to consider where a company tenant is in liquidation is the power of the liquidator to disclaim the lease.

The reasons for liquidation vary. A company that is insolvent may be wound up so that its assets can be liquidated and distributed among its creditors. Alternatively a company may wish to reconstruct or amalgamate with another and needs to be wound up for that purpose. Consequently winding up may be compulsory by the court or voluntary either by its creditors or members. The effects of each on the landlord's normal remedies for tenant default are different.

The position is to be contrasted with that of the tenant in administration or in receivership. The administrator will be looking to achieve the purposes of the administration order. The receiver will be looking to realise the assets over which he has been appointed. The liquidator, however, will be looking to realise what assets are available and in an orderly manner to distribute among the creditors in the statutory order of priority. The alternative would be each creditor pursuing its own remedy in competition with the others.

For the liquidator the process may involve selling what assets are left after any receiver has finished and/or challenging earlier transactions that have perhaps cheated creditors out of assets to which they ought to have been entitled (this aspect of reviewable disposition is dealt with elsewhere). The receiver's job finally will be to dissolve the company and have it struck off the Companies Register. In the meantime, the landlord will need to take what remedies are available depending on the type of liquidation, to retain as much of the rental income flow as possible and to reduce any potential loss.

24.1 Types of liquidations

A liquidation will either be voluntary or compulsory. If the company is solvent then it will be a member's voluntary liquidation. If the company is insolvent then it will either be a creditor's voluntary liquidation or a compulsory winding up by the court.

Member's voluntary winding up

To effect a member's voluntary winding up the directors of the company have to make a statutory declaration that it is solvent. The statutory declaration also has to comply with section 89 of the Insolvency Act 1986. The declaration is a form which in legal terms is treated as equivalent to an oath for the purposes of the law of perjury. Directors need to fix a period of not more than 12 months from the start of the winding up during which the company will pay its debts in full. To do this the directors will need to take account of contingent and prospective liabilities as well as the actual debts at the date of the declaration. This does not mean that the company itself has to be solvent: it is possible that the expectation of all debts being paid within the following 12 months is because a third-party guarantee, perhaps from associated or parent company, is available to ensure that the terms of the declaration will be met.

The concern for the landlord is to ensure that the company's proposals include dealing with the lease and this will be usually either by by way of assignment to a new tenant or, at the landlord's option, the grant of a new lease to a new tenant. In either case the landlord should take the usual precautions in enquiring as to the value and reliability of the proposed new tenant or assignee by way of references, trading accounts, rent deposit deeds and, where appropriate, guarantors. This is because when the winding up is completed, the company will be struck off the Companies Register and cease to exist. Any rights the landlord may have against the tenant in liquidation either as original tenant, current tenant or intermediate tenant will similarly cease.

Creditor's voluntary winding up

If no statutory declaration of solvency is made in accordance with section 89 of the Insolvency Act 1986 or the liquidator appointed decides that the company cannot pay its debts in full with interest as set out the declaration then the liquidation will be a creditor's voluntary winding up. If the liquidator is of such an opinion that the company cannot pay its debts as set out in section 95 of the

Insolvency Act 1986 then the liquidator has to call a meeting of the company's creditors within 28 days of forming that opinion under section 89.

When the creditors meet, the directors have to provide a statement in a prescribed form on the affairs of the company. The creditors may then nominate a person to be liquidator, but if no one is nominated then the person nominated by the shareholders is the liquidator under section 100 Insolvency Act 1986. The creditor's may also appoint up to five persons to form part of a creditor's committee (referred to in section 101 as a liquidation committee) to supervise the liquidation and to fix the liquidator's remuneration. On the appointment of the liquidator the directors' powers cease, unless the liquidation committee otherwise agreed under section 103 Insolvency Act 1986.

The landlord needs to ensure that following the appointment of a liquidator, he deals only with the liquidator and not with the director. If as landlord he receives notice of a creditors' meeting he should seek out other creditors to see if an agreement can be reached as to who should be appointed liquidator; this will enable the landlord to have some control over the liquidation of the tenant company. However, at the same time, the landlord should also review what options are available by way of forfeiture, distress and action against previous tenants or guarantors (and this is dealt with further below).

Compulsory winding up

A compulsory winding up of a tenant company will arise where a creditor or several creditors petition the court for a winding-up order. The grounds on which the tenant may be compulsory wound up are dealt with in section 122 of the Insolvency Act 1986, but the most common ground is that the company is unable to pay its debts. The inability to pay debts is defined in section 123 of the Insolvency Act 1986 to include the following:

- Where a creditor has served a statutory demand (in a prescribed form) on the company for a debt of more than £750 and it has not within three weeks paid, secured or compounded that debt to the creditor's reasonable satisfaction.
- If execution or other process is not satisfied.
- If it is shown to the satisfaction of the court that the company is unable to pay its debts as they fall due.

- If it is shown to the satisfaction of the court that the value of the company assets is less than the amount of its liabilities taking into account its contingent and prospective liabilities.

The winding-up petition is usually made by a creditor, but it can also be made by a director of the company, a contributory or the clerk of the magistrates court in relation to an unpaid fine.

In any event the court has discretion whether to make the winding-up order. The landlord's remedies are much more restricted following a compulsory winding up than in a voluntary liquidation.

24.2 The landlord's position

The liquidator's powers and the effect of the liquidation varies according to whether the liquidation is voluntary or compulsory. In the same way the landlord's remedies are affected differently by the different types of liquidation.

Effects of the liquidation

The general rule is that title to the company's assets remains with the company and this will include title to the lease. It will not vest in the liquidator unless the court makes an order to that effect under section 145 of the Insolvency Act 1986. It is unusual for a liquidator to seek such an order from the court as the liquidator has wide powers to act in the company's name under Schedule 4 to the Insolvency Act 1986.

The powers set out in Schedule 4 include the following:

- The power to bring action or other legal process in the name of the company.
- The power to carry on the business of the company where beneficial for its winding up.
- The power to sell any of the company's property by auction or contract.
- The power to raise money on the security of any of the company's assets.

The powers set out in Schedule 4 are divided between Parts I to Parts IV between the different types of liquidation as follows:

- The powers in Part I are exercisable in a creditors voluntary winding up after the first creditors meeting and with the consent of the court or the liquidation committee.
- The powers in Parts II and III are exercisable in a creditor's

voluntary winding up without any consent but only after the first creditors' meeting. This includes the power to bring and defend actions or legal proceedings and to sell the company's properties.
* The powers in Part I and II in a compulsory winding up are only exercisable with the consent of the court or the liquidation committee.
* The powers in Part III may be exercisable in a compulsory winding up at any time and without consent.

In a compulsory winding up the job for the liquidator as set out in section 143 has been to secure the assets of the company, realise and distribute such assets to the company's creditors and where there is a surplus to the persons entitled to it. In both voluntary and compulsory winding up the liquidator acts as agent of the company, but in a compulsory winding up he is an officer of the court and has to exercise the degree of skill and care of a reasonable man, but *Re Wyvern Developments Ltd* [1974] 1 WLR 1097.

Options for the liquidator

The liquidator will be concerned about whether the property has any value in the winding up and, if not, whether it is still necessary to retain the property to achieve a better realisation of the company's assets. The liquidator will also be aware that the landlord may force his hand in the decision to disclaim the lease by serving a notice to elect. The landlord will be concerned about whether the rent will be paid and, if not, whether the alternative remedies of distress or forfeiture provide adequate security for unpaid rent, while, at the same time, reviewing his options as landlord to sue the original tenant, intermediate tenant and/or guarantors.

The key aspect for the landlord is the order of priority in which the debts of the company are paid by the liquidator which, so far as they relate to the landlord, are as follows:

* The expenses of the liquidation.
* Preferential debts.
* Preferential creditors.
* Unsecured creditors.

If the liquidator opts to retain possession of the premises to carry on the company's business or to deal with the lease then he will have to pay the rent in full and it is likely that this will be treated as an expense of liquidation giving the landlord priority (subject to the rights of secured creditors).

If the liquidator has no use for the property then the landlord's options are either to force the liquidator's hand on the issue of disclaimer or to pursue the alternative remedies of distress or forfeiture.

The position on distress is as follows:

- If the tenant is in voluntary liquidation the landlord's right to levy distress is not affected although the liquidator or any contributory or creditor may apply to the court to determine any question or exercise any of the powers which might be exercised in a compulsory winding up. This will include a power to stay any distress. If a distress was started before the liquidation it may be allowed to proceed, but not otherwise.

- If the tenant is in compulsory liquidation then the position depends on whether the distress was levied before or after the commencement of the winding up. If the petition has been presented then a creditor or contributory may apply for the proceedings to be stayed under section 126. If the winding-up order had been made then the court's leave will be needed to continue the distress. If the distress is levied after the commencement of the winding up then it is void under section 128 of the Insolvency Act 1986.

The position on forfeiture is as follows:

- In a voluntary winding up the landlord's remedy of forfeiture is not affected although the liquidator, a contributory or creditor may apply to the court for a stay of proceedings under section 112.

- In a compulsory liquidation no leave of the court is required if the lease is forfeited before the winding-up order is made but after the petition is presented, but leave of the court is required when the winding-up order has been made under section 130 of the Insolvency Act 1986.

24.3 Disclaimer by the liquidator

Power to disclaim

Under the Insolvency Act 1986 (sections 178–182) a liquidator may disclaim any "onerous property", ie any unprofitable contract and any other property of the company which is unsaleable or not readily saleable or is such that it may give rise to a liability to pay money or perform any other onerous act. In the case of a lease, a mere decorating liability can make the lease "onerous": *Eyre* v *Hall*

Managing Business Tenants

[1986] 2 EGLR 95. Under the above sections leave of the court is no longer required.

However the disclaimer of any lease may not take effect unless a copy of the disclaimer has been served on the tenant, any subtenants and anyone holding a mortgage over the lease and either:

• No application for a vesting order is made with respect to that property before the end of the period of 14 days beginning with the day on which the last notice of disclaimer was served under this subsection.
• Or where such application has been made the court directs that the disclaimer shall take effect.

The liquidator is not under any duty to disclaim the lease within a fixed time-limit unless he is put on notice to disclaim by a person who is interested in the property under section 178 of the Insolvency Act 1986. Such a notice will impose a 28-day period upon the liquidator in which to elect whether or not to disclaim the lease. The form of notice is prescribed under rule 4.191 of the Insolvency Rules 1986. The effect of forcing the liquidator to elect is that he will be prevented from disclaiming the lease if:

• A person interested in the property has applied to him requiring him to elect.
• A period of 28 days has elapsed beginning with the date on which the application was made (or such longer period as the court allows) and no notice of disclaimer has been given by the liquidator to disclaim the lease.

If the liquidator fails to disclaim the lease there is a risk that the landlord will obtain priority over other creditors and the rent arrears will be treated as an expense for the whole period of the liquidation.

A landlord is a person interested in the premises for these purposes, but so also is an original tenant, an intermediate tenant and a subtenant. In particular where there is a subtenant the landlord should consider whether the better option would be to encourage the liquidator to surrender the lease rather than disclaim it. This is because the surrender of the lease would make the subtenant the immediate tenant of the landlord under section 139 Law of Property Act 1925. This may be of importance to the landlord where there is no immediate prospect of another tenant being found at a similar or greater rent. If the lease is disclaimed the subtenant will have the option of applying for a vesting order or simply walking away from the premises. The landlord may prefer to take away that option from the subtenant.

When the lease has been disclaimed the court has power on application to order that the disclaimed property (which in this case means the lease) is vested in the party making the application. The parties interested in the property may make such an application and this includes the following:

- Any person who claims an interest in the lease. This would cover the landlord, a subtenant or a mortgagee.
- Any person who is under any liability under the lease which is not discharged by the disclaimer. This would cover an original or intermediate tenant and possibly a guarantor if the terms of the guarantee extend to these circumstances.

Effect of disclaimer

The general effect of a disclaimer under section 178 of the Insolvency Act 1986 is as follows:

- The rights, interest and liabilities of the tenant company under the lease is determined from the date of the disclaimer.
- The rights or liabilities of any other person under the leases is not affected except so far as is necessary to release the company from any liability.

The effect of section 178 in relation to a lease is as follows:

- If the tenant in liquidation is the original tenant and there are no guarantors then the lease is determined.
- If the tenant in liquidation is the original tenant with a guarantor then the disclaimer in addition releases the guarantor.
- If the tenant in liquidation is an original tenant and the lease has been assigned then the original tenant's liability ends, but the assignee remains liable by privity of estate as the current tenant.
- If the tenant in liquidation is an assignee and current tenant at the same time then the original tenant's liability continues together with that of any guarantors and any prior tenants who are still linked to the landlord by privity of contract under a licence to assign.
- If the tenant in liquidation has sublet the premises then the sublease appears to end but the subtenant may apply to the court for a vesting order. In effect the subtenant remains in

possession while the sublease might have continued not in breach, provided the terms of the headlease are not otherwise: see *Re A E Realisations (1985) Ltd* [1988] 1 WLR 200.

24.4 Reviewable dispositions

The liquidator has power under the Insolvency Act 1986 to avoid certain transactions. These may arise where some creditors, including the landlord, have entered into a transaction with the company which prejudices other creditors. The type of transactions concerned include dispositions which prefer some creditors to others and transactions which are below market value. For the landlord this may be the lease itself or possibly a guarantee by the company to the landlord of another tenant's obligation. The landlord needs to aware of the types of transactions which may be avoided by the liquidator and the time-limits involved.

Transactions at an undervalue
This is defined in section 238 of the Insolvency Act 1986 and arises where:

- The company has made its transaction a gift or otherwise entered into a transaction on terms that provide for no consideration.
- The company has entered into a transaction for a consideration the value of which in money or money's worth is significantly less than that provided by the company.

The liquidator that can apply to the court for an order under section 238 to set aside that transaction and ask the court to order under section 241 that:

- Any property transferred as part of the transaction is returned to the company.
- Any proceeds of sale are returned to the company.
- Any charges given are released.

However the transaction has to be entered into during the period of six months ending with the onset of insolvency. Where the person with whom the transaction is made is connected with the company then that period is extended to two years. To be connected with a company a person might be a director or shadow director or an associate of that company, and associate is widely defined in section 435 to include, among others, that person's spouse, relative, partner or combination of any of these.

There is protection for the landlord under section 238 of the Insolvency Act 1986 if it can be shown:

• That the tenant entered into the transaction in good faith for the purpose of carrying on its business.
• That when it entered into the transaction there was a reasonable ground to believe that the transaction would benefit the company.

There is also protection for third parties like the landlord under section 241 where an interest is acquired in good faith for value and without notice of the circumstances which made it a transaction at an undervalue.

To set aside the transaction the liquidator must also show that when it was entered into by the company it was unable to pay its debts under section 123 of the Insolvency Act 1986 or became unable to pay its debts as a consequence of that transaction.

Preferences
A preference is another type of transaction, which may be set aside by the liquidator and arises where:

• The person to whom the preference is given is one of the company's creditors, sureties or guarantors.
• The company does anything or suffers anything to be done which in the event of an insolvent liquidation puts that person in a better position than he otherwise would have been in.

The same time periods under section 240 in relation to transactions at an undervalue apply to preferences and in addition the liquidator has to show that at the time of the preference the company was unable to pay its debts or became so unable as a result of that preference. The court has power to restore the position to what it would have been if the preference had not been made.

CHAPTER 25

Tenant in bankruptcy

Bankruptcy order and trustees powers
Before an individual is made bankrupt, a bankruptcy petition is presented. The bankruptcy petition may be presented on the following grounds:

- Where a creditor petitions on the grounds set out in section 267: that there is a debt exceeding the current bankruptcy level which the debtor appears either to be unable to pay or to have no reasonable prospect of being able to pay.
- Where the debtor himself petitions for his own bankruptcy on the grounds set out in section 272: that the debtor is unable to pay his debts.

If the bankruptcy petition results in an order then the official receiver is appointed receiver and manager of the property until a trustee in bankruptcy is appointed under sections 293 to 297. Under section 287 the official receiver is initially the receiver and manager of the property and the bankrupt's interest in it vests in the official receiver only if he becomes a trustee. Similarly under section 306 the bankrupt's interest in the property vests in the trustee on his appointment.

The powers of the trustee in bankruptcy (who must be a licenced insolvency practitioner) are set out in Schedule 5.

The powers described in Schedule 5 are divided between those which require the sanction of the court or the creditors' committee (including power to run the business of the tenant) and those powers which are generally available to the trustee in bankruptcy without prior consent and these include the power to deal with any property. Where a trustee has exercised power without proper consent this can be subsequently ratified under section 314 of the Insolvency Act 1986.

The immediate concern to the landlord will be whether the trustee in bankruptcy proposes to disclaim the lease; and, if so, the effect on the other remedies otherwise available for rent and other breaches of the lease.

25.1 Disclaimer
Generally
There is a general power under section 315 for the trustee to disclaim any onerous property, which includes unprofitable contracts and any other property which is unsaleable or not readily saleable, or which may give rise to a liability to pay money or perform any other onerous act. The trustee can exercise his right to disclaim even though he may have already tried to sell the property. The effect of the disclaimer is to determine the right, interest and liability of the bankrupt in the disclaimed property and discharge the trustee from all personal liability with effect from the start of the trusteeship, but does not otherwise affect the rights and liabilities of any other person. The form of notice is prescribed by rule 6.178 and form 6.61 of the Insolvency Rules. Its service and communication is covered by rule 6.179 to 6.181. However in the case of leases the further requirements in section 317 need to be followed and this includes serving a copy of the disclaimer on everyone of whom the trustee is aware as claiming under the bankrupt as subtenant or mortgagee.

The effect of the disclaimer is postponed under section 179 and 317 and in relation to the bankrupt's dwelling under section 318; the disclaimer takes effect if no application under sections 181 or 320 is made for a vesting order within 14 days of the disclaimer. However, even in those circumstances any other interested party apart from a subtenant or mortgagee is able to apply to the court for a vesting order within three months of being aware of the disclaimer under sections 181 and 320.

Effect of disclaimer on the lease
The effect of the disclaimer by the trustee in bankruptcy of the lease is as follows:
- Where the bankrupt is the original tenant and there are no guarantors, the lease simply ends in effect.
- Where the bankrupt is the original tenant with a guarantor, then the disclaimer releases the guarantor.
- Where the bankrupt is an original tenant which has assigned, the original tenant's liability ends but the assignee remains liable by privity of estate.
- Where the bankrupt is an assignee and the current tenant, the original tenant's liability continues together with that of any guarantors.

- Where the tenant has sublet, the sublease ends but the subtenant may apply to the court for a vesting order. This position should be contrasted with a surrender by the bankrupt tenant under which the subtenant becomes the direct tenant of the head landlord. This means that a trustee in bankruptcy may wish to play off, in a falling market, the respective interests of the landlord looking for a surrender and to the keep the property occupied, and the subtenant, who may want to have the option of deciding whether to apply for a vesting order or walk away from the sublease.

25.2 Insolvent landlord
Generally
The bankruptcy of the landlord does not end the landlord's obligations unless and until the trustee in bankruptcy disclaims the landlord's interest in the lease. If so, then the tenant will have to be given notice under section 317 and will be able to seek a vesting order under section 320; otherwise the lease ends.

Tenant's position
Until the trustee in bankruptcy disclaims the lease the tenant has the following options:

- To perform the covenants of which the landlord is in breach and serve notice of any breach, claiming the cost against the trustee in bankruptcy.
- To claim damages from the trustee in bankruptcy, having put him on notice to elect whether to disclaim under section 316. If the trustee does not disclaim he will have adopted the lease and so the tenant will be able to claim for damages directly from the trustee who will be indemnified from the assets (if any) remaining in the estate.
- To claim set-off in respect of the rent under section 323 for the mutual debt arising before the commencement of the bankruptcy, or to claim set-off generally for any post-bankruptcy rent as an equitable right.

25.3 Reviewable dispositions
Gifts and transactions at undervalue
The trustee in bankruptcy can apply to the court under section 339 for an order, on such terms as the court thinks fit, to set aside any transaction at an undervalue and restore the position to what it

would have been if that transaction had not been entered into.

The type of order that may be given is set out in section 342 and includes the following:

- To require any transfer of property to be revested in the trustee.
- To require the repayment of sale proceeds.
- To release or discharge any security.

The rights of third parties are also affected under section 342, although *bona fide* purchasers for value without notice of the relevant circumstances are protected under section 342(2).

A transaction at an undervalue is defined under section 339(3) as including the following transactions by a person who is subsequently made bankrupt:

- A gift or transaction on terms that provide for no consideration.
- A transaction in consideration of marriage.
- A transaction for consideration the value of which in money or moneys worth is significantly less than the value in money or moneys worth of the consideration provided by the individual with whom it is made.

The trustee in bankruptcy can apply to the court to set aside a transaction at an undervalue if it is made at the relevant time. Under section 341(1) the relevant time is during the period of five years ending with the presentation of the bankruptcy petition.

Under section 341(2) the transaction will be made at the relevant time if it is entered into between two and five years before the bankruptcy petition and if the person with whom the transaction is entered into is insolvent at that time or becomes insolvent as a consequence of that transaction. These conditions are presumed satisfied where the transaction is entered into with an associate.

The individual with whom the transaction is entered into is insolvent if either he is unable to pay this debts as and when they fall due, or the value of his assets is less than the amount of his liabilities taking into account his contingent and prospective liabilities.

Associate for these purposes is more fully defined in section 435 but includes a spouse, a relative or spouse of a relative, a partner or an employee. Further definitions of associate are set out in section 435.

Although third-party rights are protected under section 342(2) this does not apply where that third party had notice of the relevant circumstances. In effect this means that the property is frozen after a gift within the relevant time. Initially this means two years, or five years where the donor is insolvent at the time of the gift or subsequently becomes insolvent as a result of that gift. A declaration of solvency provides good evidence of the donor's status at the time of the gift, but is not beyond challenge. The usual searches will show up a bankruptcy petition and a bankruptcy order.

As far as registered land is concerned a gift is registered subject to minor interests, which includes creditors claims, under sections 20(4) and 23(5) of the Land Registration Act 1925.

As far as unregistered land is concerned the production of a gift as part of the epitome of title effectively freezes the land for the statutory period.

It may be possible to reduce the freezing period to two years with a declaration of solvency and to obtain indemnity insurance against the risk of an application under section 339.

Preferences

Section 340 provides for a trustee in bankruptcy to apply to the court to set aside a transaction where that transaction is by way of a preference. The court, as with transactions at undervalue, can make such order as it thinks fit, restoring the position to what it would have been had that preference not been made.

A transaction is a preference if it is made with a person who is one of the debtor's creditors or a surety or guarantor for any of his debts or other liabilities and where the debtor does anything which has the effect of putting that person into a position which following bankruptcy is better than the position he would have been in had the preference not been made. Preference can only be challenged by the trustee in bankruptcy if the debtor (which subsequently becomes the bankrupt) was influenced by a desire to put the individual with whom the preference was made in a better position than he would otherwise have been in. However such an intention is presumed where the preference is given to an associate. The definition of associate is, as before, more fully defined in section 345, although this is qualified in section 340(5) as excluding individuals or associates other than by reason only of being an employee of the bankrupt. The presumption that the preference is influenced by a desire to achieve the effects stated in section 340 where it is made with an associate is rebuttable by contrary evidence. Preferences for these purposes include court orders under section 340(6).

The relevant time during which a preference can be challenged is two years where the individual to whom the preference is given is an associate or connected with the bankrupt. In any other case where the preference is not a transaction at an undervalue the relevant period is six months ending with the presentation of the bankruptcy petition.

As with transactions at an undervalue there are provisions to protect third parties under section 342 where the transaction is in good faith for value and without notice of the relevant circumstances.

Transactions defrauding creditors

Section 423 deals with transactions that are at an undervalue (and similarly defined in section 423(1)) where the court is able to set aside a transaction which is both at an undervalue and designed to put assets beyond the reach of creditors.

The court can made such order as it thinks fit to restore the position as if a transaction had not been entered into and to protect the interest of the victim, but only where the purpose of a transaction is one of the following:

- To put the assets beyond the reach of a person who is making or subsequently makes a claim against the debtor.
- To prejudice otherwise the interest of such a person.

An example of an application under section 423 is seen in *Arbuthnot Leasing International Ltd* v *Havelet Leasing Ltd* [1992] 1 WLR 455. Also in *Cohan* v *Saggar* (unreported 1991) the court held that the above conditions were satisfied if the dominant purpose of the bankrupt was to achieve one of the two purposes set out above. A victim for these purposes is anyone capable of being prejudiced by the transaction at an under value.

25.4 Landlord's position

The usual remedies

The usual remedies available to the landlord with an insolvent tenant either where there are rent arrears or other breaches of the lease are as follows:

- To sue the tenant.
- To sue any original tenant, intermediate tenant and/or guarantors.
- To levy distress.

• To forfeit the lease.

Where the tenant is bankrupt these remedies are restricted by the terms of the Insolvency Act 1986 and the power of the trustee in bankruptcy to oppose proceedings and/or to disclaim the lease. However, the landlord still retains a number of remedies which are available and these are dealt with below.

Distress

The bankruptcy of the tenant does not affect the landlord's power to distrain against the goods of the tenant, which is to be contrasted with the position where the tenant is in liquidation. There is no requirement for leave of the court under section 285 for the landlord to levy distress (see *Smith, (A Bankrupt) In Re, ex parte Braintree District Council* [1989] 3 WLR 1317) and under section 347 the landlord retains the right to distrain against property comprised in the bankrupt's estate even though that property has vested in the trustee in bankruptcy.

However, while the landlord has favourable treatment under section 347 he may only distrain for a maximum of six-months' rent accruing before the bankruptcy began.

If the distress has been levied after the bankruptcy petition but before the order then the landlord must return any proceeds which exceed the amount for which he can distrain under section 347. Again this contrasts with a more complicated position that arises when a tenant is in liquidation.

In any event the landlord retains the right to prove in the bankruptcy for unpaid rent under section 347 of the Insolvency Act 1986.

Where there is an interim order against the tenant the landlord can still levy distress notwithstanding section 252 of the Insolvency Act 1986: see *McMullen* v *Cerrone* [1993] EGCS 108.

Rent and other terms

The lease vests in the trustee in bankruptcy on his appointment and that makes him personally liable for rent and other terms of the lease unless it is disclaimed: *Metropolis Estates Co Ltd* v *Wilde* [1940] 2 KB 536. However, where the trustee does disclaim the lease and has not taken on any personal liability for rent or the other terms, he will not be liable for the period during which the lease vested in him. This is because section 315 of the Insolvency

Act makes it clear that the disclaimer discharges the trustee from all personal liability with effect from the commencement of the trusteeship. It is only if the trustee fails to disclaim that he is at risk of incurring personal liability.

When the bankruptcy petition has been presented the court can stay any action for a breach of the terms of the lease or rent arrears under section 285. When the bankruptcy order is made any similiar action will require the court's leave. Any action to claim rent arrears will fail as the landlord will have the right to prove as an unsecured creditor in the bankruptcy, but without prejudice to his right to levy distress under section 347 of the Insolvency Act 1986.

Forfeiture

The general rule under section 285 of the Insolvency Act 1986 is that after the bankruptcy order has been made leave of the court is needed before any action or other legal process can be started against the bankrupt. However, it has been argued (see *Exchange Travel Agency Ltd* v *Triton Property Trust plc*) [1991] 2 EGLR 50 that if the reason for forfeiture does not involve arrears of rent or service charge then leave is not required particularly where the object of the forfeiture is not to enforce payment of any debt but to end the lease: see also *Ezekiel* v *Orakpo* [1977] QB 260.

However, if the lease is forfeited whether by court proceedings or by peaceable re-entry, the tenant in bankruptcy through the trustee will be able to apply to the court for relief (as set out above).

CHAPTER 26

Empty property

When faced with taking a property in hand there are a number of basic issues worthy of consideration, which include: security, maintenance, insurance, rates, other outgoings, short-term income opportunities and remarketing.

26.1 Security

The property should be inspected and careful attention paid to site security including, if necessary, changing of locks, boarding up of windows, etc.

Consideration should be given to regular security inspections and the deterrence of both vandals, squatters and fly traders.

26.2 Maintenance

Thought must be given to ensuring that the premises are at least wind and water tight to ensure against deterioration of the fabric.

Mundane housekeeping matters such as the draining down of water systems, the provision of background heating, if appropriate, etc must be addressed.

If the property has landscaping or grounds, then provision must be made for regular grass cutting, etc.

It is important to make routine inspections of a property that has become vacant so that any burgeoning problems can be nipped in the bud.

26.3 Insurance

Care must be taken to ensure that the property has continuous insurance cover for all perils and that it is insured to its full reinstatement value. Failure to maintain cover to the full reinstatement value can lead to a loss against a claim under the averages clause.

26.4 Rates as an outgoing

The uniform business rate (UBR) is essentially a tax on occupiers.

Where there is no occupier it generally falls to the person with the rights of occupation.

The annual liability to UBR is a product of rateable value for the hereditament multiplied by the rate in the pound.

The rateable value is the national annual rental value of the hereditament on a tenancy from year to year with effect from April 1 1988. All valuations are made at that antecedent date but can reflect material changes (in physical circumstances etc) since that date. There will be a revaluation, effective from April 1 1995, when the antecedent valuation date will be April 1 1993.

The rate in the pound is fixed annually for England and also for Wales and for Scotland.

Rates are collected by district councils and information on rateable values and rates in the pound can be obtained from them.

Vacant buildings
The liability for rates falls to the person entitled to occupation. With an empty building, if there is still a lease in place then it is the tenant who is liable for rates, otherwise it is the owner.

Under section 45 of the Local Government Finance Act 1988 the Secretary of State is given the power to make regulations relating to the rates liability in respect of unoccupied hereditaments. The Non-Domestic Rating (Un-occupied Property) Regulations 1989 cover this. The main exemptions are found in regulation 2(2):

A *First three months*
No empty rates are charged during the first three months of vacancy. To qualify for a second three-month rates holiday, the hereditament must have been re-occupied for at least six weeks.

B *Owner prohibited by law from occupying*
This might include the absence of a fire certificate as in *Tower Hamlets London Borough Council* v *Abdi* [1993] 06 EG 102.

C *Hereditament kept vacant due to action by crown etc*

D *Listed buildings*

E *Ancient monuments*

F *Industrial and storage hereditaments*
Qualifying industrial hereditaments are defined as:
Any hereditament other than a retail hereditament in relation to which all buildings comprised in the hereditament are
• Constructed or adapted for use in the course of a trade or business and

- Constructed or adapted for use for one or more of the following purposes:
  - (i)   The manufacture, repair or adaptation of goods or materials, or the subjection of goods or materials to any process;
  - (ii)   Storage (including the storage or handling of goods in the course of their distribution);
  - (iii)   The working or processing of minerals;
  - (iv)   The generation of electricity.
- G *Small hereditaments*
     Where the rateable value is below £1,000.
- H *Personal representatives*
- I   *Bankruptcy*
- J   *Trustees*
- K *Companies being wound up*
     Exception of regulation 2(2) applies where the owner is a company which is subject to a winding-up order made under the Insolvency Act 1986.
- L   *Liquidators*
     Liquidators appointed under section 112 and 145 of the Insolvency Act 1986 are exempt.

For any vacant property not in one of the above exemptions, (primarily shops, offices and leisure properties) the rate charge is at 50% of the full UBR charge for that year.

Mitigation of liability
There are several routes to investigate if faced with a rates liability for vacant property including:

- Does it qualify under one of the exemptions.
- Are there grounds to appeal against the rateable value to secure a reduction.
- Are there grounds to appeal against the description of the property in the rating list. Can the valuation officer be persuaded that a mixed commercial hereditament is primarily "a warehouse, store and premises", thus getting in to exemption F?
- Can a composite hereditament be assessed in parts – thus putting separate assessments on say offices/retail/storage so that the storage element benefits from the exemption.
- Remember that occupation of part is deemed to be occupation of the whole. If only part of a building is in use, examine whether the

empty parts can become a separate hereditament thus attracting only half rates or a total exemption.

26.5 Other outgoings

All other potential outgoings must be identified. These would include:

- *Statutory services*
  Gas, water, electricity. Do you require continuity of service or for the services to be cut off.
- *Ground rents etc*
  Payments of rents on ground leases, etc, must be maintained to avoid forfeiture when dealing with leasehold properties.

26.6 Short-term income

There are a variety of opportunities for generating short-term income depending upon the nature and location of the vacant property. These may include the licensing of shops over the Christmas shopping period to seasonal traders, the use of car parking facilities for neighbouring occupiers, short-term storage contracts, the use of large yards for Sunday markets, etc.

When entering into any agreement for short-term income, care must be taken that a tenancy with Landlord and Tenant Act protection is not inadvertently created.

26.7 Marketing

The ultimate objective with vacant property must be either to realise the asset with an open market sale or to reinstate the income stream by obtaining a worthwhile letting.

A vacant property that has been carefully maintained and monitored and which is presented in reasonable order is likely to have a greater market appeal. Care must be taken to avoid the property becoming stigmatised or labelled.

Careful attention should be paid to the choice of sale/letting agent and control maintained over the marketing tools to be adopted and the method of sale employed. In weak market conditions landlords must be flexible and prepared to offer incentive packages to attract the right calibre of tenant.

It must always be remembered that the right calibre of tenant will not only provide a secure income stream but will, given the quality of their covenant, enhance the capital value of the investment. It does not necessarily pay to take the first prospective tenant that comes along or even the tenant that makes the highest rental bid. Similar considerations apply in a freehold sale, it is the purchaser who can demonstrate the ability to proceed and the will to proceed, not necessarily the highest bidder who should be accepted.

CHECKLISTS

CHAPTER 27

On the lease/assignment

These are some of the issues for the landlord to consider on the grant or renewal of a lease or on the assignment of an existing lease to a new tenant.

Investment value
Whether there is any opportunity to improve or develop the premises prior to the tenant's occupation or as part of the renewal, so as to improve the investment value, marketability or rental value of the premises.

Alternative premises
Whether there is any opportunity for the landlord to make use of alternative premises he owns and to renegotiate terms with the tenant accordingly.

Existing lease
Whether there is any opportunity to improve on the terms of any existing lease to deal with any difficulties met in the past.

Other leases
Whether the terms of any other leases owned by the same landlord have impact on the proposed lease of the premises.

Company search
Whether a company search should be made against the tenant and if already made whether there are any points to be followed up.

References
Whether references for the tenant raise any issues that need to be followed up.

Trading accounts
Whether the trading accounts for the tenant are adequate and

reveal sufficient comfort in terms of turnover, profit, fixed assets and rent cover.

Rental deposit or personal guarantee
Whether any rent deposit or personal guarantee is needed and if so on what terms.

Withholding consent
Whether, on assignment, there are any reasonable grounds for withholding consent.

Licence to assign
Whether, on an assignment, the licence to assign includes a covenant from the tenant to observe and perform the covenants in the lease and to pay the rent through the rest of its term.

Tenant's business
Whether the tenant's business is likely to have any impact on the investment value of the premises.

Environmental damage
Whether the tenant's business is likely to have any impact on the environment and consequently increase the landlord's liability for any environmental damage.

Commercial risks
Whether the tenant's business holds any commercial risks because, for example, it is a new venture or dependant on a key man or a particular type of customer or supplier.

Security of tenure
Whether there is any scope for negotiation or trade off of security of tenure, repairing obligations, flexibility in assigning or subletting, break-clauses, rent review dates and rent.

CHAPTER 28

On the terms of the lease

These are the issues to be considered by the landlord and his property manager in negotiating the terms of the lease.

Agreement before lease
Whether an agreement before lease is needed, for example, where there are things that a tenant is to do or pre-conditions to be fulfilled before the lease is granted or assigned.

Extent of the premises
Whether an existing lease adequately defines the extent of the premises particularly in respect of the tenants repairing obligations.

Plans
Whether the landlord is to provide plans to identify the extent of the premises or works to be carried out by the tenant prior to the grant of the lease.

Rights granted
Whether there are sufficient rights granted with the premises to cover such matters as access, services, car parking, toilets, fire escapes, and other facilities.

Reserved rights
Whether the landlord has reserved adequate rights over the premises for such matters as rights of entry for inspection, repair or maintenance, rights to develop any adjoining property and rights to use service media and installations serving adjoining property.

Adjoining property
Whether the length of the term has to fit in with the leases of adjoining properties.

Reserved as rent
Whether service charge, insurance premium and other matters are reserved as rent as well as the rent itself.

Rent review terms
Whether the rent review terms give the best possible review covering such matters as upwards-only review, reference to arbitration or expert at landlord's option, the maximum hypothetical term, disregards of rent-free periods for fitting-out works, assumption of compliance by landlord with covenants, assumptions as to VAT status of tenant where relevant and any other matters covered by the current Law Society/RICS standard rent review clause.

Repairing obligation
Whether the repairing obligation of the tenant is adequate and, where relevant, includes an obligation to renew, replace or rebuild, or liability for inherent defects and consequential damage if possible and whether a schedule of condition is appropriate.

Decorating clauses
Whether the decorating clauses fit the type of building and the decorating years are at appropriate intervals.

User clause
Whether the user clause is sufficiently flexible so as not to impact on the rent review, but to maintain control over use of premises.

Assigning or subletting
Whether restrictions on assigning or subletting are adequate to control the user, but maintain rental value on review.

Alterations and improvements
Whether restrictions on alterations and improvements are adequate, for example, by prohibiting structural alterations and limiting the extent of non-structual alterations with prior consent of the landlord.

Costs
Whether the landlord can collect his costs on grant of lease and if so where the liability for VAT will lie.

Insurance
Whether insurance is to be in joint names and the terms and extent of the insurance to be maintained by the landlord.

Service charge provisions
Whether the service charge provisions cover all the services to be provided by the landlord and adequately charge the tenant.

Forfeiture clause
Whether the forfeiture clause covers all the relevant events and whether there are further provisions for rent suspension in the event of insured damage with a landlord's option to determine if reinstatement is impossible or frustrated.

Additional regulations
Whether there are additional regulations the landlord would want to impose for a shop or industrial or office premises to cover such matters as nuisance, prohibited uses, noise, overloading, security, refuse disposal and car parking.

CHAPTER 29

On rent collection

These are the points of which the landlord and the property manager needs to be aware.

Rent payment terms
Whether the lease adequately covers the rent payment terms as to frequency of payment, for example, by equal quarterly payments or monthly in advance and on what dates and whether by bankers standing order or by direct debit, with or without VAT, and with interest on late payment.

Rent collection system
Whether the landlord's rent collection system has all the relevant contact details, addresses and telephone numbers.

Demand
Whether the demand is sent out early enough for payment to be made by the due date.

Follow up
Whether any failure to pay is followed up quickly enough to identify whether late payment for this particular tenant is unusual or normal.

Remedial or pro-active steps
Whether any late payment is followed up quickly enough to take any remedial or pro-active steps in the event of late payment or breach.

When rent should not be collected
Whether the system is set up to identify when rent should not be collected, for example, to avoid waiving rights of forfeiture.

Speed
Whether any late receipt of rent by the landlord has anything to do

with the speed with which the managing agents are acting, and, if so, what steps may be taken to improve the prompt and efficient collection of rent.

CHAPTER 30

On levying distress

When looking at the issue of levying distress the landlord and his agent should consider the following.

Appropriate
Whether distress is the appropriate remedy as against other remedies such as forfeiture.

Worthwhile
Whether there are goods at the premises which are of sufficient value to make distress worthwhile.

Threat
Whether the value of the distress lies in its execution or in its threat, particularly relevant where a receiver or trustee in bankruptcy is withholding rent prior to the sale of assets of a business at the premises.

Third-party goods
Whether the tenant's business is likely to have a high proportion of third-party goods against which it may not be worth distraining.

Impact of insolvency
Whether the tenant is in administration, administrative receivership, bankruptcy or liquidation and if so the impact of each on the remedy of distress.

CHAPTER 31

On forfeiting the lease

The landlord and the property manager need to consider the following issues before enforcing forfeiture.

Reserved
Whether the right to forfeit has been reserved in the lease.

The impact of insolvency
Whether the tenant is already in administration or administrative receivership or liquidation or bankruptcy and the impact of each on the remedy of forfeiture.

The event relied upon
Whether the event relied upon as a ground for forfeiture fits the terms of the forfeiture clause in the lease.

Waiver
Whether there has been any waiver by the landlord or its agents of the right to forfeit.

Relief
Whether the tenant proposes or is likely to apply to the court for relief from forfeiture.

Section 146
Whether the forfeiture is for non-payment of rent or some other breach of the lease and if so whether the procedure under section 146 of the Law of Property Act 1925 has been followed.

CHAPTER 32

On dealing with the receiver

Where the landlord becomes aware that a receiver has been appointed for the tenant or the premises then the following issues arise.

Type
Whether the receiver is appointed over a tenant in administrative receivership or over a property in LPA receivership.

Forfeiture
Whether there are rent arrears or other breaches of the lease outstanding and, if so, whether forfeiture is available as a remedy.

Original tenant
Whether the tenant in receivership is an original tenant, if not whether action can be taken against the original tenant, previous tenant or their respective guarantors for rent arrears and other breaches of the lease.

Distress
Whether there are any assets at the property against which distress can be levied as an alternative to forfeiture.

Negotiate
Whether the receiver needs to retain the premises in the short term to achieve a sale of the business and, if so, whether levying distress will force the receivers to negotiate over any existing rent arrears.

Subtenants
Whether there are any sub-tenants at the property from whom rent can be collected directly.

CHAPTER 33

On dealing with the liquidator

Where the landlord is aware that the tenant is in liquidation the following issues arise.

Type
Whether the liquidation is voluntary or compulsory as this affects the available landlord's remedies.

Proposal
Whether the liquidator is likely to retain the property to achieve a better realisation of the companies assets and, if so, what proposals the liquidator has for existing rent or arrears.

Original tenant
Whether the tenant in liquidation is an original tenant and, if not, whether action may be taken against the previous tenants or the original tenant and/or its guarantors for breaches of the lease or rent arrears.

Distress or forfeiture
Whether the remedies of distress or forfeiture are available with or without leave of the court or, in any event, are worth pursuing at all.

Subtenants
Whether there are any subtenants and if so whether there will be any benefits in a surrender of the lease by the tenant in liquidation.

Disclaimer
Whether notice should be served on the liquidator to force his decision on the disclaimer of the lease.

CHAPTER 34

On dealing with the administrator

The appointment of administrator over a tenant company raises the following issues for the landlord and his agent.

Leave of the court
Whether leave of the court should be obtained, or the consent of the administrator, to the commencement of action against the tenant in administration or to enfroce the alterative remedies of forfeiture and distress.

Original tenants
Whether alternative action can be taken against any previous tenants or any original tenants and/or their respective guarantors.

Preserve usual remedies
Whether the landlord should try to prevent the administration order being made, so as to preserve its usual remedies as landlord.

Liquidation
Whether the landlord is able to present a petition for the liquidation of the company, if the administration order has not yet been made, and whether there are other creditors who would be interested in joining in such an application.

CHAPTER 35

On dealing with the trustee in bankruptcy

The landlord will only be concerned with the tenant in bankruptcy where the tenant is an individual but in such circumstances the issues are as follows.

Original tenant
Whether the tenant is an original tenant and, if not, whether there are prior tenants and/or guarantors who can be sued for rent arrears and/or other breaches of the lease.

Subtenants
Whether there are any sub-tenants from whom the rent can be claimed.

Disclaimer
Whether notice should be served on the trustee to force his hand on disclaimer.

Distress
Whether there are any assets at the property which may be distrained for rent arrears.

Leave of the court
Whether leave of the court should be obtained to forfeit the lease or whether, where there is a subtenant, the better option might be to consider a surrender of the intermediate lease.

Index